THE AMERICAN CLOCK

A VAUDEVILLE

Based in part on Studs Terkel's *Hard Times*

BY ARTHUR MILLER

DRAMATISTS
PLAY SERVICE
INC.

INTRODUCTION

The American Clock was begun in the early seventies and did not reach final form until its production at the Mark Taper Forum in Los Angeles in 1984, a version that in turn was movingly and sometimes hilariously interpreted in the Peter Wood production two years later at the British National Theatre. The seemingly endless changes it went through reflected my own search for something like a dramatic resolution to what, after all, was one of the vaster social calamities in history — the Great Depression of the thirties. I have no hesitation in saying that as it now stands, the work is simply as close to such a resolution as I am able to bring it, just as the experience itself remains only partially resolved in the hands of historians. For the humiliating truth about any "period" is its essential chaos, about which any generalization can be no more than just that, a statement to which many exceptions may be taken.

With all its variety, however, there were certain features of the Depression era that set it apart, for they had not existed before in such force and over such a long time. One of the most important of these to me, both as a person living through those years and as a writer contemplating them three decades afterwards, was the introduction into the American psyche of a certain unprecedented *suspense.* Through the twenties the country, for me — and I believe I was typical — floated in a a reassuring state of nature that merged boundlessly with the sea and the sky; I had never thought of it as even having a system. But the Crash forced us all to enter history willy-nilly, and everyone soon understood that there were other ways of conducting the nation's business — there simply had to be, because the one we had was so persistently not working. It was not only the radicals who were looking at the historical clock and asking how long our system could last, but people of every viewpoint. After all, they were hardly radicals who went to Washington to ask the newly inaugurated President Roosevelt to nationalize the banks, but bankers themselves who had finally confessed their inability to control their own system. The objective situation, in a word, had surfaced; people had taken on a new consciousness that had been rare in more prosperous times, and the alternatives of fascism or socialism were suddenly in the air.

Looking back at it all from the vantage of the early seventies, we seemed to have reinserted the old *tabula rasa*, the empty slate, into our heads again. Once more we were in a state of nature where no alternatives existed and nothing had grown out of anything else. Conservatism was still damning the liberal New Deal, yearning to dismantle its remaining prestige, but at the same time the Social Security system, unemployment and bank insurance, the regulatory agencies in the stock market — the whole web of rational protections that the nation relied on — were products of the New Deal. We seemed to have lost awareness of community, of what we rightfully owe each other and what we owe ourselves. There seemed a want of any historical sense. America seems constantly in flight to the future; and it is a future made much like the past, a primeval paradise with really no government at all, in which the pioneer heads alone into the unknown forest to carve out his career. The suddenness of the '29 Crash and the chaos that followed offered a pure instance of the impotance of individualist solutions to so vast a crisis. As a society we learned all over again that we are in fact dependent and vulnerable, and that mass social organization does not necessarily weaken moral fiber but may set the stage for great displays of heroism and self-sacrifice and endurance. It may also unleash, as it did in the thirties, a flood of humor and optimism that was far less apparent in seemingly happier years.

When Studs Terkel's *Hard Times* appeared in 1970, the American economy was booming, and it would be another seventeen years before the stock market collapsed to anything like the degree it had in 1929. In any case, in considering his collection of interviews with survivors of the Depression as a partial basis for a play (I would mix my own memories into it as well), I had no prophecy of doom in mind, although in sheer principle it seemed impossible that the market could keep on rising indefinitely. At bottom, quite simply, I wanted to try to show how it was and where we had come from. I wanted to give some sense of life as we lived it when the clock was ticking every day.

The idea was not, strictly speaking, my invention but a common notion of the thirties. And it was a concept that also extended outward to Europe and the Far East; Hitler was clearly preparing to destroy parliamentary governments as soon as he organized his armies, just as Franco had destroyed the Spanish Republic, and Japan was manifestly creating a new empire that must one day collide with the interests of Britain and the United States. The clock was ticking everywhere.

Difficulties with the play had to do almost totally with finding a balance between the epic elements and the intimate psychological lives of individuals and families like the Baums. My impulse is usually toward integration of meaning through significant individual action, but the striking new fact of life in the Depression era — unlike the self-sufficient, prosperous seventies — was the swift rise in the common consciousness of the social system. Uncharacteristically, Americans were looking for answers far beyond the bedroom and purely personal relationships, and so the very form of the play should ideally reflect this wider awareness. But how to unify the two elements, objective and subjective, epic and psychological? The sudden and novel impact of the Depression made people in the cities, for example, painfully conscious that thousands of farm families were being forced off their lands in the West by a combination of a collapsed market for farm goods and the unprecedented drought and dust storms. The farmers who remained operating were aware — and openly resentful — that in the cities people could not afford to buy the milk for which they could not get commercially viable prices. The social paradoxes of the collapse were so glaring that it would be false to the era to try to convey its spirit through the life of any one family. Nevertheless the feeling of a unified theatrical event evaded me until the revision for the 1984 Mark Taper production, which I believe came close to striking the balance. But it was in the British National Theatre production two years later that the play's theatrical life was finally achieved. The secret was vaudeville.

Of course the period had much tragedy and was fundamentally a trial and a frustration for those who lived through it, but no time ever created so many comedians and upbeat songs. Jack Benny, Fred Allen, W.C. Fields, Jimmy Durante, Eddie Cantor, Burns and Allen, and Ed Wynn were some of the headliners who came up in that time, and the song lyrics were most often exhilaratingly optimistic: "Love Is Sweeping the Country," "Life Is Just a Bowl of Cherries," "April in Paris," "I'm Getting Sentimental Over You," "Who's Afraid of the Big Bad Wolf?" It was, in the pop culture, a romantic time and not at all realistically harsh. The serious writers were putting out books like Nathanael West's *Miss Lonelyhearts,* Erskine Caldwell's *God's Little Acre,* Jack Conroy's *The Disinherited,* André Malraux's *Man's Fate,* Hemingway's *Winner Take Nothing,* and Steinbeck's *In Dubious Battle,* and Edward Hopper was brooding over his stark street scenes, and Reginald Marsh was painting vagrants asleep in the subways, but Broadway had O'Neill's first comedy, *Ah, Wilderness!,* and another comical version of the hard life, *Tobacco Road,* Noel Coward's *Design for Living,* the Gershwins' *Let 'Em Eat Cake,* and some of the best American farces ever written — *Room Service, Three Men on a Horse,* and *Brother Rat* among them.

In the Mark Taper production I found myself allowing the material to move through me as it wished — I had dozens of scenes by this time and was shifting them about in search of their hidden emotional as well as ideational linkages. At one point the experience brought to mind a sort of vaudeville where the contiguity of sublime and ridiculous is perfectly acceptable; in vaudeville an imitation of Lincoln doing the Gettysburg Address could easily be followed by Chinese acrobats. So when subsequently Peter Wood asked for my feeling about the style, I could call the play a vaudeville with an assurance born of over a decade of experimentation. He took the hint and ran with it, tossing up the last shreds of a realistic approach, announcing from the opening image that the performance was to be epic and declarative.

Out of darkness, in a brash music hall spotlight, a baseball pitcher appears and tosses a ball from hand to glove as he gets ready on the mound. The other characters saunter on singing snatches of songs of the thirties, and from somewhere in the balcony a man in a boater and striped shirt, bow tie and gartered sleeves — Ted Quinn — whistles "I Found a Million-Dollar Baby in a Five-and-Ten-Cent Store." At one side of the open stage, a five-piece jazz band plays in full view of the audience (impossible in the penurious New York Theatre), and the sheer festivity of the occasion is already established.

The most startling, and I think wonderful, invention of all was the treatment of the character Theodore K. Quinn. This was the actual name of a neighbor of mine, son of a Chicago railroad labor organizer, who had worked himself up from a poor Chicago law student to the vice-presidency of General Electric. The president of GE, Quinn's boss through most of the twenties, was Gerard Swope, a word-famous capitalist and much quoted social thinker, who decided as the thirties dawned that Quinn was to succeed him on his retirement. Quinn, in charge of the consumer products division of the company, had frequently bought up promising smaller manufacturers for Swope, incorporating their plants into the GE giant, but had developed a great fear that this process of cartelization must end in the destruction of democracy itself. Over the years his rationalization had been that he was only taking orders — although in fact it was on his judgment that Swope depended as to which companies to pick up. Then the excuses were threatened by his elevation to the presidency, an office with dictatorial powers at the time. As he would tell me, "Above the president of General Electric stood only God."

The real Ted Quinn had actually been president of GE for a single day, at the end of which he put in his resignation. "I just couldn't stand being the Lord High Executioner himself," he once said to me. He went on to open an advisory service for small businesses and made a good fortune at it. During World War II he was a dollar-a-year head of the Small Business Administration in Washington, seeing to it that the giant concerns did not gobble up all the available steel. Particularly close to his heart was the Amana company, a cooperative.

Quinn also published several books, including *Giant Business, Threat to Democracy* and *Unconscious Public Enemies,* his case against GE-type monopolies. These, along with his anti-monopoly testimony before congressional committees, got him obliterated from the roster of former GE executives, and the company actually denied — to journalist Matthew Josephson, who at my behest made an inquiry in 1972 — that he had ever so much as worked for GE. However, in the course of time a film director friend of mine who loved to browse in flea markets and old bookstores came on a leather-covered daily diary put out by GE as a gift for its distributors, circa 1930, in which the company directors are listed, and Theodore K. Quinn is right there as vice-president for consumer sales. The fact is that it was he who, among a number of other innovations, conceived of the compact electric refrigerator as a common consumer product, at a time when electric refrigeration was regarded as a purely commercial item, the behemoth used in restaurants, hotels, and the kitchens of wealthy estates.

From the big business viewpoint Quinn's central heresy was that democracy basically depended on a large class of independent entrepreneurs who would keep the market competitive. His fear was that monopoly, which he saw spreading in the American economy despite superficial appearances of competition, would end by crippling the system's former ingenuity and its capacity to produce high-quality goods at reasonable prices. A monopoly has little need to improve its product when it has little need to compete. (First Communist China then Gorbachev's Russia would be grappling with a very similar dilemma in the years to come.) He loved to reel off a long list of inventions, from the jet engine to the zipper, that were devised by independent inventors rather than corporations and their much advertised laboratories: "The basic things we use and are famous for were conceived in the back of a garage." I knew him in the fifties, when his populist vision was totally out of fashion, and maybe, I feared, an out-of-date relic of a bygone America. But I would hear it again in the seventies and even more loudly in the eighties as a muscle-bound American industrial machine, wallowing for generations in a continental market beyond the reach of foreign competition, was caught flat-footed by German and Japanese competitors. Quinn was a successful businessman interested in money and production, but his vision transcended the market to embrace the nature of the democratic system for which he had a passion, and which he thought doomed if Americans did not understand the real threats to it. He put it starkly once: "It may be all over, I don't know — but I don't want to have to choose between fascism and socialism, because neither one can match a really free, competitive economy and the political liberties it makes possible. If I do have to choose, it'll be socialism, because it harms the people less. But neither one is the way I'd want to go."

Perhaps it was because the style of the National Theatre production was so unashamed in its presentational declarativeness that the Ted Quinn role was given to David Schofield, a tap dancer with a brash Irish mug, for Quinn was forever bragging about — and mocking — his love of soft-shoe dancing. And so we had long speeches about the dire consequences of business monopoly delivered by a dancer uncorking a most ebullient soft-shoe all over the stage, supported by some witty jazz played openly before our eyes by a deft band. As Quinn agonizes over whether to accept the presidency of GE, a phone rings at the edge of the stage; plainly, it is as the new president that he must answer it. He taps his way over to it, lifts the receiver, and simply places it gently on the floor and dances joyously away.

It was in the National Theatre that I at last heard the right kind of straightforward epic expressiveness, joyful and celebratory rather than abashed and veiled, as economic and political — which is to say epic — subjects were in the mouths of the characters. In this antic yet thematically precise spirit, accompanied by some forty songs out of the period, the show managed to convey the *seriousness* of the disaster that the Great Depression was, and at the same time its human heart.

There was one more invention that I particularly prized. Alone in her Brooklyn house, Rose Baum sits at the piano, bewildered and discouraged by the endless Depression, and plays some of the popular ballads of the day, breaking off now and then to muse to herself about the neighborhood, the country, her family, her fading hopes. The actress sat at a piano whose keyboard faced the audience, and simply held her hands suspended over the keys while the band pianist a few years away played the romantic thirties tunes. Gradually a triple reality formed such as I have rarely witnessed in the theatre: first, the objective stage reality of the band pianist playing, but somehow magically directed by Rose's motionless hands over her keyboard; and simultaneously, *the play's memory* of this lost past that we are now discovering again; and finally, the middle-aged actress herself seeming, by virtue of her motionless hands suspended over the keys, to be recalling this moment from her very own life. The style, in short, had fused emotion and conscious awareness, overt intention and subjective feeling — the aim in view from the beginning, more than a decade before.

THE AMERICAN CLOCK was revised in 1984 and opened at the Cottesloe Theatre, of the National Theatre, in London, on August 15, 1986. It later moved to the Olivier Theatre of the National Theatre and opened on December 18, 1986. It was directed by Peter Wood; the set design was by Timothy O'Brien; the costume design was by Stephen Lewis; the lighting design was by Robert Bryan; the musical arrangements were by Robert Lockhart; the sound design was by Paul Groothuis; the production manager was Michael Cass Jones and the stage manager was Ernest Hall. The cast was as follows:

ARTHUR ROBERTSON .... Barrie Ingham
CLARENCE, ISAAC .... Tommy Eytie
MOE BAUM .... Michael Bryant
ROSE BAUM .... Sara Kestelman
LEE BAUM .... Neil Daglish
GRANDPA .... Peter Gordon
FANNY MARGOLIES, CHARLESTON DANCER .... Sally Dexter
SIDNEY MARGOLIES, CHARLESTON DANCER,
    HENRY TAYLOR, RYAN .... Barry James
LUCILLE, DIANA MORGAN,
    HARRIET TAYLOR .... Roz Clifton
DORIS GROSS, CHARLEY, EDIE .... Eve Adam
JOEY, BROADWAY TONY, FARMER,
    STANISLAUS .... Steven Law
FRANK, SERVANT, LOUIS BANKS, RUDY,
    TOLAND .... Okon Jones
DR. ROSMAN, GRANDMA TAYLOR .... Edna Dore
JESSE LIVERMORE, IOWA SHERIFF, BUSH ..... Alan Haywood
WILLIAM DURANT, JUDGE BRADLEY,
    DUGAN .... John Normington
ARTHUR CLAYTON, BREWSTER, MR. GRAHAM,
    RALPH .... Adam Norton
MRS. TAYLOR, MISS FOWLER, GRACE .... Judith Coke
DAUGHTERS .... Annabel Mednick, Valerie Minifie
SERVANTS .... Tommy Eytie, Marsha Hunt, Okon Jones,
                                    Ellen Thomas, Major Wiley

FRANK HOWARD, THEODORE K. QUINN,
     MISSISSIPPI SHERIFF, KAPUSH ....David Schofield
FARMER, CHUCK... Nicholas Donovan
BIDDERS .... Robert Ralph, Paul Stewart
MARATHON DANCERS .... Roz Clifton, Nicholas Donovan,
                              Annabel Mednick, Adam Norton
ISABEL, IRENE... Marsha Hunt
MUSICIANS................................ Robert Lockhart, David Roach,
          Roy Babbington, Michael Gregory, Peter Pettinger

THE AMERICAN CLOCK was first produced at the Harold
Clurman Theatre, in New York City, and opened at the Spoleto
Festival's Dockside Theatre in Charlestown, South Carolina, on
May 24, 1980. It was later produced at the Biltmore Theatre, in
New York City, on November 20, 1980.

CHARACTERS

THEODORE K. QUINN
LEE BAUM
ROSE BAUM, Lee's Mother
MOE BAUM, Lee's father
ARTHUR A. ROBERTSON
CLARENCE, a shoeshine man
FRANK, the Baums' chauffeur
FANNY MARGOLIES, Rose's sister
GRANDPA, Rose's father
DR. ROSMAN
JESSE LIVERMORE, WILLIAM DURANT, ARTHUR
    CLAYTON, financiers
TONY, a speakeasy owner
DIANA MORGAN
HENRY TAYLOR, a farmer
IRENE, a middle-aged black woman
BANKS, a black veteran
JOE, a boyhood friend of Lee's
MRS. TAYLOR, Henry's wife
HARRIET TAYLOR, their daughter
BREWSTER, CHARLEY, farmers
JUDGE BRADLEY
FRANK HOWARD, an auctioneer
MISS FOWLER, Quinn's secretary
GRAHAM, a New York *Times* Reporter
SIDNEY MARGOLIES, Fanny's son
DORIS GROSS, the landlady's daughter
RALPH, RUDY, students
ISABEL, a prostitute
ISAAC, a black café proprietor
RYAN, a federal relief supervisor
MATTHEW R. BUSH, GRACE, KAPUSH, DUGAN, TOLAND,
    LUCY, people at the relief office
EDIE, a comic-strip artist

LUCILLE, Rose's niece
STANISLAUS, a seaman
BASEBALL PLAYER
WAITER
THIEF
FARMERS
BIDDERS
SHERIFF
DEPUTIES
MARATHON DANCERS
WELFARE WORKER
SOLDIERS

THE AMERICAN CLOCK

ACT ONE

The set is a flexible area for actors. The actors are seated in a choral area onstage and return to it when their scenes are over. The few pieces of furniture required should be openly carried on by the actors. An impression of a surrounding vastness should be given, as though the whole country were really the setting, even as the intimacy of certain scenes is provided for. The background can be sky, clouds, space itself or an impression of the geography of the United States.

A small jazz band onstage plays a song like "Million-Dollar Baby"* as a baseball pitcher enters, tossing a ball from hand to glove. Quinn begins to whistle a song like "Million-Dollar Baby"* from the balcony. Now he sings, and the rest of the company joins in, gradually coming onstage. All are singing by the end of the verse. All form in positions onstage. The band remains onstage throughout the play.

ROSE. By the summer of 1929 ...

LEE. I think it's fair to say that nearly every American ...

MOE. Firmly believed that he was going to get ...

COMPANY. Richer and richer ...

MOE. Every year.

ROBERTSON. The country knelt to a golden calf in a blanket of red, white, and blue. *(He walks to Clarence's shoeshine box.)* How you making out, Clarence?

CLARENCE. Mr. Robertson, I like you to lay another ten dol-

* See Special Note on copyright page.

lars on that General Electric. You do that for me?

ROBERTSON. How much stock you own, Clarence?

CLARENCE. Well, this ten ought to buy me a thousand dollars' worth, so altogether I guess I got me about hundred thousand dollars in stock.

ROBERTSON. And how much cash you got home?

CLARENCE. Oh, I guess about forty, forty-five dollars.

ROBERTSON. *(Slight pause.)* All right, Clarence, let me tell you something. But I want you to promise me not to repeat it to anyone.

CLARENCE. I never repeat a tip you give me, Mr. Robertson.

ROBERTSON. This isn't quite a tip, this is what you might call an untip. Take all your stock, and sell it.

CLARENCE. Sell! Why, just this morning in the paper Mr. Andrew Mellon say the market's got to keep goin' up. *Got* to!

ROBERTSON. I have great respect for Andrew Mellon, Clarence, know him well, but he's up to his eyebrows in this game — he's got to say that. You sell, Clarence, believe me.

CLARENCE. *(Drawing himself up.)* I never like to criticize a customer, Mr. Robertson, but I don't think a man in your position ought to be carryin' on that kind of talk! Now you take this ten, sir, put it on General Electric for Clarence.

ROBERTSON. I tell you something funny, Clarence.

CLARENCE. What's that, sir?

ROBERTSON. You sound like every banker in the United States.

CLARENCE. Well, I should hope so!

ROBERTSON. Yeah, well ... bye-bye. *(He exits. Clarence exits with his shoeshine box. The company exits singing and humming a song like "Million-Dollar Baby"*; Quinn sings the final line. Light rises on Rose at the piano, dressed for an evening out. Two valises stand C.)*

ROSE. *(Playing piano under speech).* Now sing, darling, but don't forget to breathe — and then you'll do your homework.

LEE. *(Starts singing a song like "I Can't Give You Anything But Love,"* then speaks over music.)* Up to '29 it was the age of be-

---

* See Special Note on copyright page.

lief. How could Lindbergh fly the Atlantic in that tiny little plane? He believed. How could Babe Ruth keep smashing those homers? He believed. Charley Paddock, "The World's Fastest Human," raced a racehorse ... and won! Because he believed. What I believed at fourteen was that my mother's hair was supposed to flow down over her shoulders. And one afternoon she came into the apartment ... *(Rose, at piano, sings a line of a song like "I Can't Give You Anything But Love."*)* ... and it was short! *(Rose and Lee sing the last line together.)*

ROSE. *(Continuing to play, speaking over music.)* I personally think with all the problems there was never such a glorious time for anybody who loved to play or sing or listen or dance to music. It seems to me every week there was another marvelous song. What's the matter with you? *(Lee can only shake his head — "nothing.")* Oh, for God's sake! Nobody going to bother with long hair anymore. All I was doing was winding it up and winding it down ...

LEE. It's *okay!* I just didn't think it would ever ... happen.

ROSE. But why can't there be something new!

LEE. But why didn't you *tell* me?

ROSE. Because you would do exactly what you're doing now — carrying on like I was some kind of I-don't-know-what! Now stop being an idiot and *sing!* *(Lee starts singing a song like "On the Sunny Side of the Street."*)* You're not breathing, dear. *(Moe enters carrying a telephone, joins in song. Lee continues singing under dialogue.)* Rudy Vallee is turning green. *(Frank enters in a chauffeur's uniform.)*

MOE. *(Into phone.)* Trafalgar five, seven-seven-one-one. *(Pause.)* Herb? I'm just thinking, maybe I ought to pick up another five hundred shares of General Electric. *(Pause.)* Good. *(He hangs up.)*

FRANK. Car's ready, Mr. Baum. *(Frank chimes in with Lee on the last line of a song like "Sunny Side of the Street."* Then Lee sits on the floor, working on his crystal set.)*

ROSE. *(To Frank.)* You'll drop us at the theatre and then take my father and sister to Brooklyn and come back for us after the show. And don't get lost, please.

* See Special Note on copyright page.

FRANK. No, I know Brooklyn. *(He exits with the baggage. Fanny enters — Rose's sister.)*

FANNY. *(Apprehensively.)* Rose ... listen ... Papa really doesn't want to move in with us. *(A slow turn with rising eyebrows from Moe; Rose is likewise alarmed.)*

ROSE. *(To Fanny.)* Don't be silly, he's been with us six months.

FANNY. *(Fearfully, voice lowered.)* I'm telling you ... he is not happy about it.

MOE. *(Resoundingly understating the irony.)* He's not happy.

FANNY. *(To Moe.)* Well, you know how he loves space, and this apartment is so roomy.

MOE. *(To Lee.)* He bought himself a grave, you know. It's going to be in the cemetery on the aisle. So he'll have a little more room to move around,...

ROSE. Oh, stop it.

MOE. ... get in and out quicker.

FANNY. *(Innocently.)* Out of a grave?

ROSE. He's kidding you, for God's sake!

FANNY. Oh! *(To Rose.)* I think he's afraid my house'll be too small; you know, with Sidney and us and the one bathroom. And what is he going to do with himself in Brooklyn? He never liked the country.

ROSE. Fanny, dear, make up your mind — he's going to *love* it with you.

MOE. Tell you, Fanny — maybe we should *all* move over to your house and he could live here with an eleven-room apartment for himself, and we'll send the maid every day to do his laundry ...

FANNY. He's brushing his hair, Rose, but I know he's not happy. I think what it is, he still misses Mama, you see.

MOE. Now *that's* serious — a man his age still misses his mother ...

FANNY. No, *our* mother — *Mama. (To Rose, almost laughing, pointing at Moe.)* He thought Papa misses his own mother!

ROSE. No, he didn't, he's kidding you!

FANNY. Oh, you...! *(She swipes at Moe.)*

ROSE. *(Walking her to the doorway.)* Go hurry him up. I don't want to miss the first scene of this show; it's Gershwin, it's supposed to be wonderful.

FANNY. See, what it is, something is always happening here ...

MOE. *(Into phone.)* Trafalgar five, seven-seven-one-one.

FANNY. ... I mean with the stock market and the business.... Papa just loves all this! *(Grandpa appears, in a suit, with a cane; very neat, proper — and very sorry for himself. Comes to a halt, already hurt.)*

MOE. *(To Grandpa.)* See you again soon, Charley!

FANNY. *(Deferentially.)* You ready, Papa?

MOE. *(On phone.)* Herb?... Maybe I ought to get rid of my Worthington Pump. Oh ... thousand shares? And remind me to talk to you about gold, will you? *(Pause.)* Good. *(He hangs up.)*

FANNY. *(With Rose, getting Grandpa into his coat.)* Rose'll come every few days, Papa ...

ROSE. Sunday we'll all come out and spend the day.

GRANDPA. Brooklyn is full of tomatoes.

FANNY. No, they're starting to put up big apartment houses now; it's practically not the country anymore. *(In a tone of happy reassurance.)* On some streets there's hardly a tree! *(To Rose, of her diamond bracelet.)* I'm looking at that bracelet! Is it new?

ROSE. For my birthday.

FANNY. It's gorgeous.

ROSE. He gave exactly the same one to his mother.

FANNY. She must be overjoyed.

ROSE. *(With a cutting smile, to Moe.)* Why not?

GRANDPA. *(Making a sudden despairing announcement.)* Well? So I'm going! *(With a sharp tap of his cane on the floor, he starts off.)*

LEE. Bye-bye, Grandpa!

GRANDPA. *(Goes to Lee, offers his cheek, gets his kiss, then pinches Lee's cheek.)* You be a good boy. *(He strides past Rose, huffily snatches his hat out of her hand, and exits.)*

MOE. There goes the boarder. I lived to see it!

ROSE. *(To Lee.)* Want to come and ride with us?

LEE. I think I'll stay and work on my radio.

ROSE. Good, and go to bed early. I'll bring home all the music from the show, and we'll sing it tomorrow. *(She kisses Lee.)* Good night, darling. *(She swings out in her furs.)*

MOE. *(To Lee.)* Whyn't you get a haircut?

LEE. I did, but it grew back, I think.

MOE. *(Realizing Lee's size.)* Should you talk to your mother about college or something?

LEE. Oh, no, not for a couple of years.

MOE. Oh. Okay, good. *(He laughs and goes out, perfectly at one with the world. Robertson appears, walks over to the couch, and lies down. Dr. Rosman appears and sits in a chair behind Robertson's head.)*

ROBERTSON. Where'd I leave off yesterday?

DR. ROSMAN. Your mother had scalded the cat. *(Pause.)*

ROBERTSON. There's something else, Doctor. I feel a conflict about saying it ...

DR. ROSMAN. That's what we're here for.

ROBERTSON. I don't mean in the usual sense. It has to do with money.

DR. ROSMAN. Yes?

ROBERTSON. Your money.

DR. ROSMAN. *(Turns down to him, alarmed.)* What about it?

ROBERTSON. *(Hesitates.)* I think you ought to get out of the market.

DR. ROSMAN. Out of the market!

ROBERTSON. Sell everything.

DR. ROSMAN. *(Pauses, raises his head to think, then speaks carefully.)* Could you talk about the basis for this idea? When was the first time you had this thought?

ROBERTSON. About four months ago. Around the middle of May.

DR. ROSMAN. Can you recall what suggested it?

ROBERTSON. One of my companies manufactures kitchen utensils.

DR. ROSMAN. The one in Indiana?

ROBERTSON. Yes. In the middle of May all our orders stopped.

DR. ROSMAN. Completely?

ROBERTSON. Dead stop. It's now the end of August, and they haven't resumed.

DR. ROSMAN. How is that possible? The stock keeps going up.

ROBERTSON. Thirty points in less than two months. This is

20

what I've been trying to tell you for a long time now, Doctor — the market represents nothing but a state of mind. *(He sits up.)* On the other hand, I must face the possibility that this is merely my personal fantasy ...

DR. ROSMAN.   Yes, your fear of approaching disaster.

ROBERTSON.   But I've had meetings at the Morgan Bank all week, and it's the same in almost every industry — it's not just my companies. The warehouses are overflowing, we can't move the goods, that's an objective fact.

DR. ROSMAN.   Have you told your thoughts to your colleagues?

ROBERTSON.   They won't listen. Maybe they can't afford to — we've been tossing the whole country onto a crap table in a game where nobody is ever supposed to lose!... I sold off a lot two years ago, but when the market opens tomorrow I'm cashing in the rest. I feel guilty for it, but I can't see any other way.

DR. ROSMAN.   Why does selling make you feel guilty?

ROBERTSON.   Dumping twelve million dollars in securities could start a slide. It could wipe out thousands of widows and old people.... I've even played with the idea of making a public announcement.

DR. ROSMAN.   That you're dumping twelve million dollars? That could start a slide all by itself, couldn't it?

ROBERTSON.   But it would warn the little people.

DR. ROSMAN.   Yes, but selling out quietly might not disturb the market quite so much. You *could* be wrong, too.

ROBERTSON.   I suppose so. Yes.... Maybe I'll just sell and shut up. You're right. I could be mistaken.

DR. ROSMAN.   *(Relieved.)* You probably are — but I think I'll sell out anyway.

ROBERTSON.   Fine, Doctor. *(He stands, straightens his jacket.)* And one more thing. This is going to sound absolutely nuts, but ... when you get your cash, don't keep it. Buy gold.

DR. ROSMAN.   You can't be serious.

ROBERTSON.   Gold bars, Doctor. The dollar may disappear with the rest of it. *(He extends his hand.)* Well, good luck.

DR. ROSMAN.   Your hand is shaking.

ROBERTSON.   Why not? Ask any two great bankers in the

United States and they'd say that Arthur A. Robertson had lost his mind. *(Pause.)* Gold bars, Doctor ... and don't put them in the bank. In the basement. Take care, now. *(He exits. A bar. People in evening dress seated morosely at tables. An atmosphere of shock and even embarrassment.)*

LIVERMORE.   About Randolph Morgan. Could you actually see him falling?

TONY.   Oh, yeah. It was still that blue light, just before it gets dark? And I don't know why, something made me look up. And there's a man flyin' spread-eagle, falling through the air. He was right on top of me, like a giant! *(He looks down.)* And I look. I couldn't believe it. It's Randolph!

LIVERMORE.   Poor, poor man.

DURANT.   Damned fool.

LIVERMORE.   I don't know — I think there is a certain gallantry.... When you lose other people's money as well as your own, there can be no other way out.

DURANT.   There's always a way out. The door.

TONY.   Little more brandy, Mr. Durant?

LIVERMORE.   *(Raising his cup.)* To Randolph Morgan. *(Durant raises his cup.)*

TONY.   Amen here. And I want to say something else — everybody should get down on their knees and thank John D. Rockefeller.

LIVERMORE.   Now you're talking.

TONY.   Honest to God, Mr. Livermore, didn't that shoot a thrill in you? I mean, there's a *man* — to come out like that with the whole market falling to pieces and say, "I and my sons are buying six million dollars in common stocks." I mean, that's a bullfighter.

LIVERMORE.   He'll turn it all around, too.

TONY.   Sure he'll turn it around, because the man's a capitalist, he knows how to put up a battle. You wait, tomorrow morning it'll all be shootin' up again like Roman candles! *(Enter Waiter, who whispers in Tony's ear.)* Sure, sure, bring her in. *(Waiter hurries out. Tony turns to the two financiers.)* My God, it's Randolph's sister.... She don't know yet. *(Enter Diana, a young woman of elegant ease.)* How do you do, Miss Morgan, come in, come in. Here, I got a nice table for you.

DIANA. *(All bright Southern belle.)* Thank you!

TONY. Can I bring you nice steak? Little drink?

DIANA. I believe I'll wait for Mr. Robertson.

TONY. Sure. Make yourself at home.

DIANA. Are you the ... *famous* Tony?

TONY. That's right, miss.

DIANA. I certainly am thrilled to meet you. I've read all about this marvelous place. *(She looks around avidly.)* Are all these people literary?

TONY. Well, not all, Miss Morgan.

DIANA. But this is the speakeasy F. Scott Fitzgerald frequents, isn't it?

TONY. Oh, yeah, but tonight is very quiet with the stock market and all, people stayin' home a lot the last couple days.

DIANA. Is that gentleman a writer?

TONY. No, miss, that's Jake the Barber, he's in the liquor business.

DIANA. And these? *(She points to Durant and Livermore. Durant, having overheard, stands.)*

TONY. Mr. Durant, Miss Morgan. Mr. Livermore, Miss Morgan.

DIANA. *(In a Southern accent, to the audience.)* The name of Jesse Livermore was uttered in my family like the name of a genius! A Shakespeare, a Dante of corporate finance. *(Clayton, at the bar, picks up a phone.)*

LEE. *(Looking on from choral area.)* And William Durant ... he had a car named after him, the Durant Six.

MOE. *(Beside Lee.)* A *car*? Durant had control of General Motors, for God's sake.

DIANA. Not *the* Jesse Livermore?

LIVERMORE. Afraid so, yes!

DIANA. Well, I declare! And sitting here just like two ordinary millionaires!

LEE. Ah, yes, the Great Men. The fabled High Priests of the never-ending Boom.

DIANA. This is certainly a banner evening for me!... I suppose you know Durham quite well.

LIVERMORE. Durham? I don't believe I've ever been there.

DIANA.   But your big Philip Morris plant is there. You do still own Philip Morris, don't you?

LIVERMORE.   Oh, yes, but to bet on a horse there's no need to ride him. I never mix in business. I am only interested in stocks.

DIANA.   Well, that's sort of miraculous, isn't it, to own a place like that and never've seen it! My brother's in brokerage — Randolph Morgan?

LIVERMORE.   I dealt with Randolph when I bought the controlling shares in IBM. Fine fellow.

DIANA.   But I don't understand why he'd be spending the night in his office. The market's closed at night, isn't it? *(Both men shift uneasily.)*

DURANT.   Oh, yes, but there's an avalanche of selling orders from all over the country, and they're working round the clock to tally them up. The truth is, there's not a price on anything at the moment. In fact, Mr. Clayton over there at the end of the bar is waiting for the latest estimates.

DIANA.   I'm sure something will be done, won't there? *(She laughs.)* They've cut off our telephone!

LIVERMORE.   How's that?

DIANA.   It seems that Daddy's lived on loans the last few months and his credit stopped. I had no idea! *(She laughs.)* I feel like a figure in a dream. I sat down in the dining car the other day, absolutely famished, and realized I had only forty cents! I am surviving on chocolate bars! *(Her charm barely hides her anxiety.)* Whatever has become of all the money?

LIVERMORE.   You mustn't worry, Miss Morgan, there'll soon be plenty of money. Money is like a shy bird: the slightest rustle in the trees and it flies for cover. But money cannot bear solitude for long, it must come out and feed. And that is why we must all speak positively and show our confidence.

ROSE.   *(From choral area.)* And they were nothing but pickpockets in a crowd of innocent pilgrims.

LIVERMORE.   With Rockefeller's announcement this morning the climb has probably begun already.

ROBERTSON.   *(From choral area.)* Yes, but they also believed.

TAYLOR.   *(From choral area.) What* did they believe?

24

IRENE and BANKS. *(From choral area, echoing Taylor.)* Yeah, what did they believe?

ROBERTSON. Why, the most important thing of all — that talk makes facts!

DURANT. If I were you, Miss Morgan, I would prepare myself for the worst.

LIVERMORE. Now, Bill, there is no good in that kind of talk.

ROBERTSON. And they ended up believing it themselves!

DURANT. It's far more dreamlike than you imagine, Miss Morgan.

MOE. There they are, chatting away, while the gentleman at the end of the bar ...

DURANT. ... That gentleman ... who has just put down the telephone is undoubtedly steeling himself to tell me that I have lost control of General Motors.

DIANA. What! *(Clayton, at the bar, has indeed put down the phone, has straightened his vest, and is now crossing to their table.)*

DURANT. *(Watching him approach.)* If I were you, I'd muster all the strength I have, Miss Morgan. Yes, Clayton?

CLAYTON. If we could talk privately, sir ...

DURANT. Am I through?

CLAYTON. If you could borrow for two or three weeks ...

DURANT. From whom?

CLAYTON. I don t know, sir.

DURANT. *(Standing.)* Good night, Miss Morgan. *(She is looking up at him, astonished.)* How old are you?

DIANA. Nineteen.

DURANT. I hope you will look things in the face, young lady. Shun paper. Paper is the plague. Good luck to you. *(He turns to go.)*

LIVERMORE. We have to talk, Bill ...

DURANT. Nothing to say, Jesse. Go to bed, old boy. It's long past midnight.

MOE. *(Trying to recall.)* Say ... didn't Durant end up managing a bowling alley in Toledo, Ohio?

CLAYTON. *(Nods.)* Dead broke.

LIVERMORE. *(Turns to Clayton, adopting a tone of casual challenge.)* Clayton ... what's Philip Morris going to open at, can they

25

tell?

CLAYTON.   Below twenty. No higher. If we can find buyers at all.

LIVERMORE.   *(His smile gone.)* But Rockefeller. Rockefeller ...

CLAYTON.   It doesn't seem to have had any effect, sir. *(Livermore stands. Pause.)* I should get back to the office, sir, if I may. *(Livermore is silent.)* I'm very sorry, Mr. Livermore. *(Clayton exits. Diana is moved by the excruciating look coming onto Livermore's face.)*

DIANA.   Mr. Livermore?...

ROBERTSON.   *(Entering.)* Sorry I'm late, Diana. How was the trip? *(Her expression turns him to Livermore. He goes to him.)* Bad, Jesse?

LIVERMORE.   I am wiped out, Arthur.

ROBERTSON.   *(Trying for lightness.)* Come on, now, Jesse, a man like you has always got ten million put away somewhere.

LIVERMORE.   No, no. I always felt that if you couldn't have *real* money, might as well not have any. Is it true what I've heard, that you sold out in time?

ROBERTSON.   Yes, Jesse. I told you I would.

LIVERMORE.   *(Slight pause.)* Arthur, can you lend me five thousand dollars?

ROBERTSON.   Certainly. *(He sits, removes one shoe. To audience.)* Five weeks ago, on his yacht in Oyster Bay, he told me he had four hundred and eighty million dollars in common stocks.

LIVERMORE.   What the hell are you doing? *(Robertson removes a layer of five thousand-dollar bills from the shoe and hands Livermore one as he stands. Livermore stares down at Robertson's shoes.)* By God. Don't you believe in anything?

ROBERTSON.   Not much.

LIVERMORE.   Well, I suppose I understand that. *(He folds the bill.)* But I can't say that I admire it. *(He pockets the bill, looks down again at Robertson's shoes, and shakes his head.)* Well, I guess it's your country now. *(He turns like a blind man and goes out.)*

ROBERTSON.   Not long after, Jesse Livermore sat down to a good breakfast in the Sherry-Netherland Hotel and, calling for an envelope, addressed it to Arthur Robertson, inserted a note for five thousand dollars, went into the washroom, and shot himself.

DIANA. *(Staring after Livermore, then turning to Robertson.)* Is Randolph ruined too?

ROBERTSON. *(Taking her hand.)* Diana ... Randolph is dead. *(Pause.)* He ... he fell from his window. *(Diana stands, astonished. Irene sings a song like "Tain't Nobody's Bizness"* from choral area. Fadeout.)*

ROSE. *(Calling as she enters.)* Lee? Darling?

LEE. *(Takes a bike from prop area and rides on, halting before her.)* How do you like it, Ma!

ROSE. What a beautiful bike!

LEE. It's a Columbia Racer! I just bought it from Georgie Rosen for twelve dollars.

ROSE. Where'd you get twelve dollars?

LEE. I emptied my savings account. But it's worth way more!...

ROSE. Well, I should say! Listen, darling, you know how to get to Third Avenue and Nineteenth Street, don't you?

LEE. Sure, in ten minutes

ROSE. *(Taking a diamond bracelet from her bag.)* This is my diamond bracelet. *(She reaches into the bag and brings out a card.)* And this is Mr. Sanders' card and the address. He's expecting you; just give it to him, and he'll give you a receipt.

LEE. Is he going to fix it?

ROSE. No, dear. It's a pawnshop. Go. I'll explain sometime.

LEE. Can't I have an idea? What's a pawnshop?

ROSE. Where you leave something temporarily and they lend you money on it, with interest. I'm going to leave it the rest of the month, till the market goes up again. I showed it to him on Friday, and we're getting a nice loan on it.

LEE. But how do you get it back?

ROSE. You just pay back the loan plus interest. But things'll pick up in a month or two. Go on, darling, and be careful! I'm so glad you bought that bike.... It's gorgeous!

LEE. *(Mounting his bike.)* Does Papa know?

ROSE. Yes, dear. Papa knows ... *(She starts out as Joey hurries on.)*

JOEY. Oh, hiya, Mrs. Baum.

* See Special Note on copyright page.

ROSE. Hello, Joey.... Did you get thin?

JOEY. Me? *(He touches his stomach defensively.)* No, I'm okay. *(To Lee as well, as he takes an eight-by-ten photo out of an envelope.)* See what I just got? *(Rose and Lee look at the photo.)*

ROSE. *(Impressed.)* Where did you get that!

LEE. How'd you get it autographed?

JOEY. I just wrote to the White House.

LEE. *(Running his finger over the signature.)* Boy ... look at that, huh? "Herbert Hoover"!

ROSE. What a human thing for him to do! What did you write him?

JOEY. Just wished him success ... you know, against the Depression.

ROSE. *(Wondrously.)* Look at that! You're going to end up a politician, Joey. *(She returns to studying the photo.)*

JOEY. I might. I like it a lot.

LEE. But what about dentistry?

JOEY. Well, either one.

ROSE. Get going, darling. *(She exits, already preoccupied with the real problem. Lee mounts his bike.)*

LEE. You want to shoot some baskets later?

JOEY. What about now?

LEE. *(Embarrassed.)* No ... I've got something to do for my mother. Meet you on the court in an hour. *(He starts off.)*

JOEY. *(Stopping him.)* Wait, I'll go with you, let me on! *(He starts to mount the crossbar.)*

LEE. I can't, Joey.

JOEY. *(Sensing some forbidden area, surprised.)* Oh!

LEE. See you on the court. *(Lee rides off. Joey examines the autograph and mouths silently, "Herbert Hoover..." He shakes his head proudly and walks off.)*

ROBERTSON. *(From choral area.)* To me ... it's beginning to look like Germany in 1922, and I'm having real worries about the banks. There are times when I walk around with as much as twenty-five, thirty thousand dollars in my shoes. *(Frank enters in a chauffeur's uniform, a lap robe folded over his arm. Moe enters, stylishly dressed in a fur-collared overcoat, as though on a street.)*

FRANK. Morning, Mr. Baum. Got the car nice and warmed up

for you this morning, sir. And I had the lap robe dry-cleaned.

MOE. *(Showing Frank a bill.)* What is that, Frank?

FRANK. Oh. Looks like the garage bill.

MOE. What's that about tires on there?

FRANK. Oh, yes, sir, this is the bill for the new tires last week.

MOE. And what happened to those tires we bought six weeks ago?

FRANK. Those weren't very good, sir, they wore out quick — and I want to be the first to admit that!

MOE. But twenty dollars apiece and they last six weeks?

FRANK. That's just what I'm telling you, sir — they were just no good. But these ones are going to be a whole lot better, though.

MOE. Tell you what, Frank ...

FRANK. Yes, sir — what I mean, I'm giving you my personal guarantee on this set, Mr. Baum.

MOE. I never paid no attention to these things, but maybe you heard of the market crash? The whole thing practically floated into the ocean, y'know.

FRANK. Oh, yes, sir, I certainly heard about it.

MOE. I'm glad you heard about it, because I heard a *lot* about it. In fact, what you cleared from selling my tires over the last ten years ...

FRANK. Oh, no, sir! Mr. Baum!

MOE. Frank, lookin' back over the last ten years, I never heard of that amount of tires in my whole life since I first come over from Europe a baby at the age of six. That is a lot of tires, Frank; so I tell ya what we're gonna do now, you're going to drive her over to the Pierce Arrow showroom and leave her there, and then come to my office and we'll settle up.

FRANK. But how are you going to get around!

MOE. I'm a happy man in a taxi, Frank.

FRANK. Well, I'm sure going to be sorry to leave you people.

MOE. Everything comes to an end, Frank, it was great while it lasted. No hard feelings. *(He shakes Frank's hand.)* Bye-bye.

FRANK. But what ... what am I supposed to do now?

MOE. You got in-laws?

FRANK. But I never got along with them.

MOE.   You should've. *(He hurries off, calling.)* Taxi!

FRANK.   *(Cap in hand, throws down lap robe and walks off aimlessly.)* Damn! *(Irene enters with a pram filled with junk and sings a few lines of a song like "Tain't Nobody's Bizness,"* unaccompanied. She picks up robe and admiringly inspects it. Then.)*

IRENE.   You got fired, you walked away to nothing; no unemployment insurance, no Social Security — just the in-laws and fresh air. *(She tosses the robe in with her junk. Fadeout.)*

ROSE.   Still ... it was very nice in a certain way. On our block in Brooklyn a lot of married children had to move back with the parents, and you heard babies crying in houses that didn't have a baby in twenty years. But of course the doubling up could also drive you crazy ... *(With hardly a pause, she turns to Grandpa, who is arriving center with canes and hatboxes. He drops the whole load on the floor.)* What are *you* doing?

GRANDPA.   *(Delivering a final verdict.)* There's no room for these in my closet ...

ROSE.   For a few *canes?*

GRANDPA.   And what about my hats? You shouldn't have bought such a small house, Rose.

ROSE.   *(Of the canes.)* I'll put them in the front-hall closet.

GRANDPA.   No, people step on them. And where will I put my hats?

ROSE.   *(Trying not to explode.)* Papa, what do you want from me? We are doing what we can do!

GRANDPA.   One bathroom for so many people is not right! You had three bathrooms in the apartment, and you used to look out the window, there was the whole New York. Here ... listen to that street out there, it's a Brooklyn cemetery. And this barber here is *very* bad — look what he did to me. *(He shows her.)*

ROSE.   Why? It's beautiful. *(She brushes some hairs straight.)* It's just a little uneven ...

GRANDPA.   *(Pushing her hand away.)* I don't understand, Rose

---

— why does he declare bankruptcy if he's going to turn around and pay his debts?

ROSE.   For his reputation.

GRANDPA.   His reputation! He'll have the reputation of a fool! The reason to go bankrupt is *not* to pay your debts!

ROSE.   (*Uncertain herself.*) He wanted to be honorable.

GRANDPA.   But that's the whole beauty of it! He should've asked me. When I went bankrupt I didn't pay *nobody!*

ROSE.   (*Deciding.*) I've got to tell you something, Papa. From now on, I wish you ...

GRANDPA.   (*Helping her fold a bed sheet.*) And you'll have to talk to Lee — he throws himself around in his bed all night, wakes me up ten times, and he leaves his socks on the floor.... Two people in that bedroom is too much, Rose.

ROSE.   I don't want Moe to get aggravated, Papa. (*He is reached, slightly glances at her.*) He might try to start a new business, so he's nervous, so please, don't complain, Papa. Please?

GRANDPA.   What did I say?

ROSE.   Nothing. (*Suddenly she embraces him guiltily.*) Maybe I can find an umbrella stand someplace.

GRANDPA.   I was reading about this Hitler ...

ROSE.   Who?

GRANDPA.   ... He's chasing all the radicals out of Germany. He wouldn't be so bad if he wasn't against the Jews. But he won't last six months.... The Germans are not fools. When I used to take Mama to Baden-Baden this time of year ...

ROSE.   How beautiful she was.

GRANDPA.   ... one time we were sitting on the train ready to leave for Berlin. And suddenly a man gallops up calling out my name. So I says, "Yes, that's me!" And through the window he hands me my gold watch and chain: "You left it in your room, mein Herr." Such a thing could only happen in Germany. This Hitler is finished.

ROSE.   (*Of the canes.*) Please.... Put them back in your closet, heh? (*He starts to object.*) I don't want Moe to get mad, Papa! (*She cuts the rebellion short and loads him with his canes and hat boxes.*)

GRANDPA.   (*Muttering.*) Man don't even know how to go bank-rupt. (*He exits. Lee appears on his bike — but dressed now for win-*

ter. He dismounts and parks the bike just as Rose lies back in the chair.)

LEE. Ma! Guess what!

ROSE. What?

LEE. Remember I emptied my bank account for the bike?

ROSE. So?

LEE. The bank has just been closed by the government! It's broke! There's a whole mob of people in the street yelling where's their money! They've got cops and everything! There is no more money in the bank!

ROSE. You're a genius!

LEE. Imagine!... I could have lost my twelve dollars!... Wow!

ROSE. That's wonderful. *(She removes a pearl choker.)*

LEE. Oh, Ma, wasn't that Papa's wedding present?

ROSE. I hate to, but ...

LEE. What about Papa's business! Can't he ...

ROSE. He put too much capital in the stock market, dear — it made more there than in his business. So now ... it's not there anymore. *(A thief swiftly appears and rides off on the bike.)* But we'll be all right. Go. You can have a jelly sandwich when you come back. *(Lee stuffs the pearls into his pants as he approaches where the bike was; he looks in all directions, his bones chilling. He runs in all directions and finally comes to a halt, breathless, stark horror in his face. As though sensing trouble, Rose walks over to him.)* Where's your bike? *(He can't speak.)* They stole your bike? *(He is immobile.)* May he choke on his next meal.... Oh, my darling, my darling, what an awful thing. *(He sobs once but holds it back. She, facing him, tries to smile.)* So now you're going to have to walk to the hockshop like everybody else. Come, have your jelly sandwich.

LEE. No, I'd like to see if I can trot there — it'd be good for my track. By the way, I've almost decided to go to Cornell, I think. Cornell or Brown.

ROSE. *(With an empty congratulatory exclamation.)* Oh!... Well, there's still months to decide. *(Rose and Lee join the company as they stand up to sing the Iowa Hymn, Verse 1: "We gather together to ask the Lord's blessing, He chastens and hastens His will to make known: The wicked oppressing now cease from distressing, Sing praises to His name: He forgets not His own." The hymn music continues under the following.)*

32

ROBERTSON. Till then, probably most people didn't think of it as a system.

TAYLOR. It was more like nature.

MRS. TAYLOR. Like weather; had to expect bad weather, but it always got good again if you waited. And so we waited. And it didn't change. *(She is watching Taylor as he adopts a mood of despair and slowly sits on his heels.)* And we waited some more and it never changed. You couldn't hardly believe that the day would come when the land wouldn't give. Land always gives. But there it lay, miles and miles of it, and there was us wanting to work it, and couldn't. It was like a spell on Iowa. We was all there, and the land was there waitin', and we wasn't able to move. *(The hymn ends.)* Amen. *(Brewster, followed by Farmers, comes front and calls to the crowd in the audience's direction.)*

BREWSTER. Just sit tight, folks, be startin' in a few minutes.

FARMER 1. *(Hitting his heels together.)* Looks like snow up there.

FARMER 2. *(Laughs.)* Even the weather ain't workin'. *(Low laughter in the crowd.)*

BREWSTER. *(Heading over to Taylor.)* You be catchin' cold sitting on the ground like that, won't you, Henry?

TAYLOR. Tired out. Never slept a wink all night. Not a wink. *(Mrs. Taylor appears carrying a big coffeepot, accompanied by Harriet, her fifteen-year-old daughter, who has a coffee mug hanging from each of her fingers.)*

MRS. TAYLOR. You'll have to share the cups, but it's something hot anyway.

BREWSTER. Oh, that smells good, lemme take that, ma'am. *(She gives the coffeepot to Brewster and comes over to Taylor. Harriet hands out the cups.)*

MRS. TAYLOR. *(Sotto voce, irritated and ashamed.)* You can't be sitting on the ground like that, now come on! *(She starts him to his feet.)* It's a auction — anybody's got a right to come to a auction.

TAYLOR. There must be a thousand men along the road — they never told me they'd bring a thousand men!

MRS. TAYLOR. Well, I suppose that's the way they do it.

TAYLOR. They got guns in those trucks!

MRS. TAYLOR. *(Frightened herself.)* Well, it's too late to stop 'em

33

now. So might as well go around and talk to people that come to help you.

CHARLEY. *(Rushing on.)* Brewster! Where's Brewster!

BREWSTER. *(Stepping forward from the crowd.)* What's up, Charley?

CHARLEY. *(Pointing off.)* Judge Bradley! He's gettin' out of the car with the auctioneer! *(Silence. All look to Brewster.)*

BREWSTER. Well ... I don't see what that changes. *(Turning to all.)* I guess we're gonna do what we come here to do. That right? *(The crowd quietly agrees: "Right," "Stick to it, Larry," "No use quittin' now," etc. Enter Judge Bradley, sixty, and Mr. Frank Howard, the auctioneer. The silence spreads.)*

JUDGE BRADLEY. Good morning, gentlemen. *(He looks around. There is no reply.)* I want to say a few words to you before Mr. Howard starts the auction. *(He walks up onto a raised platform.)* I have decided to come here personally this morning in order to emphasize the gravity of the situation that has developed in the state. We are on the verge of anarchy in Iowa, and that is not going to help anybody. Now, you are all property owners, so you —

BREWSTER. Used to be, Judge, used to be!

JUDGE BRADLEY. Brewster, I will not waste words; there are forty armed deputies out there. *(Slight pause.)* I would like to make only one point clear — I have levied a deficiency judgment on this farm. Mr. Taylor has failed to pay what he owes on his equipment and some of his cattle. A contract is sacred. The National Bank has the right to collect on its loans. Now then, Mr. Howard will begin the auction. But he has discretionary power to decline any unreasonable bid. I ask you again, obey the law. Once law and order go down, no man is safe. Mr. Howard?

MR. HOWARD. *(With a clipboard in hand, climbs onto the platform.)* Well, now, let's see. We have here one John Deere tractor and combine, three years old, beautiful condition. *(Three Bidders enter, and the crowd turns to look at them with hostility as they come to a halt.)* I ask for bids on the tractor and combine.

BREWSTER. Ten cents!

MR. HOWARD. I have ten cents. *(His finger raised, he points*

from man to man in the crowd.) I have ten cents, I have ten cents
... *(He is pointing toward the Bidders, but they are looking around at
the crowd in fear.)*
BIDDER 1.   Five hundred.
JUDGE BRADLEY.   *(Calling.)* Sheriff, get over here and protect
these men! *(The Sheriff and four Deputies enter and edge their way
in around the three Bidders. The deputies carry shotguns.)*
MR. HOWARD.   Do I hear five hundred dollars? Do I hear
five ...
BIDDER 1.   Five hundred!
MR. HOWARD.   Do I hear six hundred?
BIDDER 2.   Six hundred!
MR. HOWARD.   Do I hear seven hundred?
BIDDER 3.   Seven hundred! *(Disciplined and quick, the Farmers
grab the Deputies and disarm them; a shotgun goes off harmlessly.)*
JUDGE BRADLEY.   Brewster! Great God, what are you doing!
*(Brewster has pinned the Judge's arms behind him, and another man
lowers a noose around his neck.)*
BREWSTER.   *(To Deputies.)* You come any closer and we're
gonna string him up! You all get back on that road or we string
up the Judge! So help me Christ, he goes up if any one of you
deputies interferes with this auction! Now, let me just clear up
one thing for you, Judge Bradley ...
TAYLOR.   Let him go, Brewster — I don't care anymore, let
them take it!
BREWSTER.   Just sit tight, Henry, nobody's takin' anything.
That is all over, Judge. Mr. Howard, just to save time, why don't
you take a bid on the whole place? Do that, please?
MR. HOWARD.   *(Turns to the crowd, his voice shaking.)* I ... I'll
hear bids on ... everything. Tractor and combine, pair of mules
and wagon, twenty-six cows, eight heifers, farm and outbuildings,
assorted tools ... and so forth. Do I hear ...
BREWSTER.   One dollar.
MR. HOWARD.   *(Rapidly.)* I hear one dollar. One dollar, one
dollar?... *(He looks around.)* Sold for one dollar.
BREWSTER.   *(Handing him a dollar.)* Now, will you just sign that
receipt, please? *(Mr. Howard scribbles and hands him a receipt.
Brewster leaps off the platform, goes to Taylor, and gives him the receipt.)*

Henry? Whyn't you go along now and get to milkin'. Let's go, boys. *(He waves to the crowd, and his men follow him out. Judge Bradley, removing the noose, comes down off the platform and goes over to Taylor, who is staring down at the receipt.)*

JUDGE BRADLEY.   Henry Taylor? You are nothing but a thief! *(Taylor cringes under the accusation. The Judge points to the receipt.)* That is a crime against every law of God and man! And this isn't the end of it, either! *(He turns and stalks out.)*

HARRIET.   Should we milk 'em, Papa?

MRS. TAYLOR.   Of course we milk 'em — they're ours. *(But she needs Taylor's compliance.)* Henry?

TAYLOR.   *(Staring at the receipt.)* It's like I stole my own place. *(Near tears, humiliated, Taylor moves into darkness with his wife. The Farmers disperse.)*

ROBERTSON.   *(From choral area.)* Nobody knows how many people are leaving their hometowns, their farms and cities, and hitting the road. Hundreds of thousands, maybe millions of internal refugees, Americans transformed into strangers. *(Banks enters in army cap, uniform jacket and jeans, carrying his little bundle of clothes and a cooking pot.)*

BANKS.

> I still hear that train.
> Still hear that long low whistle.
> Still hear that train, yeah.

(He imitates train whistle: Whoo-ooo! He sings the first verse of a song like "How Long?,"* then speaks over music, which continues.) Nineteen twenty-nine was pretty hard. My family had a little old cotton farm, McGehee, Arkansas. But a man had to be on the road — leave his wife, his mother — just to try to get a little money to live on. But God help me, I couldn't get anything, and I was too ashamed to send them a picture, all dirty and ragged and hadn't shaved. Write a postcard: "Dear Mother, doin' wonderful and hope you're all fine." And me sleepin' on a Los Angeles sidewalk under a newspaper. And my ma'd say, "Oh, my son's in Los Angeles, he's doin' pretty fair." *(He grins.)* Yeah ... "all the

* See Special Note on copyright page.

36

way on the Santa Fe." So hungry and weak I begin to see snakes through the smoke, and a white hobo named Callahan got a scissors on me, wrapped me 'tween his legs — otherwise I'd have fell off into a cornfield there. But except for Callahan there was no friendships in the hobo jungle. Everybody else was worried and sad-lookin', and they was evil to each other. I still hear that long low whistle ... *whoo-ooo! (Banks sings the second verse of a song like "How Long?"* Then the music changes into a song like "The Joint is Jumpin.'"* Marathon Dancers enter, half asleep, some about to drop. They dance. Fadeout. Light comes up on Moe in an armchair. Lee enters with college catalogues.)*

MOE.   When you say three hundred dollars tuition ... Lee!

LEE.   That's for Columbia. Some of these others are cheaper.

MOE.   That's for the four years.

LEE.   Well, no, that's one year.

MOE.   Ah. *(He lies back in the chair and closes his eyes.)*

LEE.   *(Flipping a page of a catalogue.)* Minnesota here is a hundred and fifty, for instance. And Ohio State is about the same, I think. *(He turns to Moe, awaiting his reaction.)* Pa? *(Moe is asleep.)* He always got drowsy when the news got bad. And now the mystery of the marked house began. Practically every day you'd see the stranger coming down the street, poor and ragged, and he'd go past house after house, but at our driveway he'd make a turn right up to the back porch and ask for something to eat. Why us? *(Taylor appears at one side of the stage in mackinaw, farm shoes, and peaked hunter's cap, a creased paper bag under his arm. Looking front, he seems gaunt, out of his element; now he rings the doorbell. Nothing happens. Then Lee goes to the "door.")* Yes?

TAYLOR.   *(Shyly, still an amateur at the routine.)* Ah ... sorry to be botherin' you on a Sunday and all.

ROSE.   *(Enters in housedress and apron, wiping her hands on a dish towel.)* Who is that, dear? *(She comes to the door.)*

LEE.   This is my mother.

TAYLOR.   How-de-do, ma'am, my name is Taylor, and I'm just passing by, wondering if you folks have any work around the

---

* See Special Note on copyright page.

place ...

MOE. *(Waking up suddenly.)* Hey! The bell rang! *(He sees the conclave.)* Oh ...

ROSE. *(Ironically.)* Another one looking for work!

TAYLOR. I could paint the place or fix the roof, electrical, plumbing, masonry, gardening ... I always had my own farm, and we do all that, don't you know. I'd work cheap ...

ROSE. Well, we don't need any kind of ...

MOE. Where you from?

TAYLOR. State of Iowa.

LEE. *(As though it's the moon.)* Iowa!

TAYLOR. I wouldn't hardly charge if I could have my meals, don't you know.

MOE. *(Beginning to locate Taylor in space.)* Whereabouts in Iowa?

ROSE. My sister's husband comes from Cleveland.

MOE. No, no, Cleveland is nowhere near. *(To Taylor.)* Whereabouts?

TAYLOR. You know Styles?

MOE. I only know the stores in the big towns.

TAYLOR. *(Giving a grateful chuckle.)* Well! I never expected to meet a ... *(He suddenly gets dizzy, breaks off, and reaches for some support. Lee holds his arm, and he goes down like an elevator and sits there.)*

ROSE. What's the matter?

MOE. Mister?

LEE. I'll get water! *(He rushes out.)*

ROSE. Is it your heart?

TAYLOR. 'Scuse me ... I'm awful sorry ... *(He gets on his hands and knees as Lee enters with a glass of water and hands it to him. He drinks half of it, returns the glass.)* Thank you, sonny.

ROSE. *(Looks to Moe, sees his agreement, gestures within.)* He better sit down.

MOE. You want to sit down? *(Taylor looks at him helplessly.)* Come, sit down. *(Lee and Moe help him to a chair, and he sits.)*

ROSE. *(Bending over to look into his face.)* You got some kind of heart?

TAYLOR. *(Embarrassed, and afraid for himself now.)* Would you be able to give me something to eat? *(The three stare at him; he*

looks up at their shocked astonishment and weeps.)
ROSE.   You're *hungry?*
TAYLOR.   Yes, ma'am. *(Rose looks at Moe whether to believe this.)*
MOE.   *(Unnerved.)* Better get him something.
ROSE.   *(Hurrying out immediately.)* Oh, my God in heaven!
MOE.   *(Now with a suspicious, even accusatory edge.)* What're you doing, just going around?...
TAYLOR.   Well, no, I come east when I lost the farm.... They was supposed to be hiring in New Jersey, pickers for the celery? But I only got two days.... I been to the Salvation Army four, five times, but they only give me a bun and a cup of coffee yesterday ...
LEE.   You haven't eaten since *yesterday?*
TAYLOR.   Well, I generally don't need too much ...
ROSE.   *(Entering with a tray, bowl of soup, and bread.)* I was just making it, so I didn't put in the potatoes yet ...
TAYLOR.   Oh, beets?
ROSE.   That's what you call borscht.
TAYLOR.   *(Obediently.)* Yes, ma'am. *(He wastes no time, spoons it up. They all watch him: their first hungry man.)*
MOE.   *(Skeptically.)* How do you come to lose a farm?
TAYLOR.   I suppose you read about the Farmers' Uprisin' in the state couple months ago?
LEE.   I did.
MOE.   *(To Lee.)* What uprising?
LEE.   They nearly lynched a judge for auctioning off their farms. *(To Taylor, impressed.)* Were you in *that?*
TAYLOR.   Well, it's all over now, but I don't believe they'll be auctioning any more farms for a while, though. Been just terrible out there.
ROSE.   *(Shaking her head.)* And I thought they were all Republicans in Iowa.
TAYLOR.   Well, I guess they all are.
LEE.   Is that what they mean by radical, though?
TAYLOR.   Well ... it's like they say — people in Iowa are practical. They'll even go radical if it seems like it's practical. But as soon as it stops being practical they stop being radical.
MOE.   Well, you probably all learned your lesson now.

LEE. Why! He was taking their homes away, that judge!

MOE. So you go in a court and lynch him?

LEE. But ... but it's all *wrong*, Pa!

ROSE. Shh! Don't argue ...

LEE. *(To Rose.)* But *you* think it's wrong, don't you? Suppose they came and threw us out of *this* house?

ROSE. I refuse to think about it. *(To Taylor.)* So where do you sleep?

MOE. *(Instantly.)* Excuse me. We are not interested in where you sleep, Mr. ... what's your name?

TAYLOR. Taylor. I'd be satisfied with just my meals if I could live in the basement ...

MOE. *(To Taylor, but half addressing Rose.)* There is no room for another human being in this house, y'understand? Including the basement. *(He takes out two or three bills.)*

TAYLOR. I wasn't asking for charity ...

MOE. I'm going to loan you a dollar, and I hope you're going to start a whole new life. Here ... *(He hands Taylor the bill, escorting him to the door.)* And pay me back, but don't rush. *(He holds out his hand.)* Glad to have met you, and good luck.

TAYLOR. Thanks for the soup, Mrs. ...

ROSE. Our name is Baum. You have children?

TAYLOR. One's fifteen, one's nine. *(He thoughtfully folds the dollar bill. Grandpa enters, eating a plum.)*

ROSE. Take care of yourself, and write a letter to your wife.

TAYLOR. Yes, I will. *(To Moe.)* Goodbye, sir ...

MOE. *(Grinning, tipping his finger at Taylor.)* Stay away from rope.

TAYLOR. Oh, yeah, I will ... *(He exits.)*

LEE. *(Goes out on the periphery and calls to him as he walks away.)* Goodbye, Mr. Taylor!

TAYLOR. *(Turns back, waves.)* Bye, sonny! *(He leaves. Lee stares after him, absorbing it all.)*

GRANDPA. Who was that?

MOE. He's a farmer from Iowa. He tried to lynch a judge, so she wanted him to live in the cellar.

GRANDPA. What is a farmer doing here?

ROSE. He went broke, he lost everything.

GRANDPA. Oh. Well, he should borrow.

MOE. *(Snaps his fingers to Lee.)* I'll run down the street and tell him! He got me hungry. *(To Rose.)* I'm going down the corner and get a chocolate soda.... What do you say, Lee?

LEE. I don't feel like it.

MOE. Don't be sad. Life is tough, what're you going to do? Sometimes it's not as tough as other times, that's all. But it's always tough. Come, have a soda.

LEE. Not now, Pa, thanks. *(He turns away.)*

MOE. *(Straightens, silently refusing blame.)* Be back right away. *(He strolls across the stage, softly, tonelessly whistling, and exits. Grandpa, chewing, the plum pit in his hand, looks around for a place to put it. Rose sees the inevitable and holds out her hand.)*

ROSE. *(Disgusted.)* Oh, give it to me. *(Grandpa drops the pit into her palm, and she goes out with it and the soup plate.)*

LEE. *(Still trying to digest.)* That man was starving, Grandpa.

GRANDPA. No, no, he was hungry but not starving.

LEE. He was, he almost fainted.

GRANDPA. No, that's not starving. In Europe they starve, but here not. Anyway, couple weeks they're going to figure out what to do, and you can forget the whole thing.... God makes one person at a time, boy — worry about yourself. *(Fadeout.)*

ROBERTSON. His name is Theodore K. Quinn. *(Music begins — a song like "My Baby Just Cares for Me"* — and Quinn, with boater and cane, sings and dances through Robertson's speech.)* The greatest Irish soft-shoe dancer ever to serve on a board of directors. They know him at Lindy's, they love him at Twenty-one. High up on top of the American heap sits Ted Quinn, hardly forty years of age in 1932 ...

QUINN. *(Continues singing, then breaks off and picks up the phone.)* Ted Quinn. Come over, Arthur, I've got to see you. But come to the twenty-ninth floor.... I've got a new office.

ROBERTSON. *(Looking around, as at a striking office.)* All this yours?

* See Special Note on copyright page.

QUINN.   Yup. You are standing on the apex, the pinnacle of human evolution. From that window you can reach out and touch the moustache of Almighty God.

ROBERTSON.   *(Moved, gripping Quinn's hand.)* Ted! *Ted!!*

QUINN.   Jesus, don't say it that way, will ya?

ROBERTSON.   President of General Electric!

QUINN.   I'm not sure I want it, Arthur. *(Robertson laughs sarcastically.)* I'm not, goddammit! I never expected Swope to pick me — never!

ROBERTSON.   Oh, go on, you've been angling for the presidency the last five years.

QUINN.   No! I swear not. I just didn't want anybody else to get it ... *(Robertson laughs.)* Well, that's not the same thing!... Seriously, Arthur, I'm scared. I don't know what to do. *(He looks around.)* Now that I'm standing here, now that they're about to paint my name on the door ... and the *Times* sending a reporter ...

ROBERTSON.   *(Seriously.)* What the hell's got into you?

QUINN.   *(Searching in himself.)* I don't know.... It's almost like shame.

ROBERTSON.   For *what?* It's that damned upbringing of yours, that anarchist father ...

QUINN.   The truth is, I've never been comfortable with some of the things we've done.

ROBERTSON.   But why suddenly after all these years ...

QUINN.   It's different taking orders and being the man who gives them.

ROBERTSON.   I don't know what the hell you are talking about. *(Pause. For Quinn it is both a confession and something he must bring out into the open. But he sustains his humor.)*

QUINN.   I had a very unsettling experience about eighteen months ago, Arthur. Got a call from my Philadelphia district manager that Frigidaire was dropping the price on their boxes. So I told him to cut ours. And in a matter of weeks they cut, we cut, they cut, we cut, till I finally went down there myself. Because I was damned if I was going to get beat in Philadelphia ... and I finally cut our price right down to our cost of production. Well — ting-a-ling-a-ling, phone call from New York: "What the hell is going on down there?" Gotta get down to Wall Street and have a meeting with the money boys.... So there we are, about ten of us, and I look across the blinding glare of that teakwood table, and lo and behold, who is facing me but Georgy Fairchild, head of sales for Frigidaire. Old friends, Georgy and I, go way back together, but he *is* Frigidaire, y'know — what the hell is he doing in a GE meeting?... Well, turns out that both companies are owned by the same money. And the word is that Georgy and Quinn are going to cut out this nonsense and get those prices up to where they belong. (*He laughs.*) Well, I tell you, I was absolutely flabbergasted. Here I've been fightin' Georgy from Bangkok to the Bronx, layin' awake nights thinkin' how to outfox him — hell, we were like Grant and Lee with thousands of soldiers out to destroy each other, and it's suddenly like all these years I'd been shellin' my own men! (*He laughs.*) It was farcical.

ROBERTSON. It's amazing. You're probably the world's greatest salesman, and you haven't an ounce of objectivity ...

QUINN. Objectivity! Arthur, if I'm that great a salesman — which I'm far from denying — it's because I believe; I believe deeply in the creative force of competition.

ROBERTSON. Exactly, and GE is the fastest-growing company in the world because ...

QUINN. (*Loves* this point.) ... because we've had the capital to buy up one independent business after another.... It's haunting me, Arthur — thousands of small businesses are going under every week now, and we're getting bigger and bigger every day. What's going to become of the independent person in this country once everybody's sucking off the same tit? How can there be an America without Americans — people not beholden to some enormous enterprise that'll run their souls?

ROBERTSON. Am I hearing what I think? (*Quinn is silent.*) Ted? You'd actually resign?

QUINN. If I did, would it make any point to you at all? If I made a statement that ...

ROBERTSON. What statement can you possibly make that won't call for a return to the horse and buggy? The America you love

43

is cold stone dead in the parlor, Ted. This is a corporate country; you can't go back to small personal enterprise again.

QUINN.   A corporate country!... Jesus, Arthur, what a prospect! *(Miss Fowler enters.)*

MISS FOWLER.   The gentleman from the *Times is* waiting, Mr. Quinn ... unless you'd like to make it tomorrow or ...

QUINN.   *(Slight pause.)* No, no — it has to be now or never. Ask him in. *(She exits.)* Tell me the truth, Arthur, do I move your mind at all?

ROBERTSON.   Of course I see your point. But you can't buck the inevitable. *(Graham enters with Miss Fowler.)*

MISS FOWLER.   Mr. Graham.

QUINN.   *(Shakes hands, grinning.)* Glad to meet you.... My friend Mr. Robertson.

GRAHAM.   *(Recognizing the name.)* Oh, yes, how do you do?

ROBERTSON.   Nice to meet you. *(To Quinn, escaping.)* I'll see you later ...

QUINN.   No, stay ... I'll only be a few minutes ...

ROBERTSON.   I ought to get back to my office.

QUINN.   *(Laughs.)* I'm still the president, Arthur — stay! I want to feel the support of your opposition. *(Robertson laughs with Quinn, glancing uneasily at Graham, who doesn't know what's going on.)* I'll have to be quick, Mr. Graham. Will you sit down?

GRAHAM.   I have a few questions about your earlier life and background. I understand your father was one of the early labor organizers in Chicago.

QUINN.   Mr. Graham, I am resigning.

GRAHAM.   Beg your pardon?

QUINN.   Resigning, I said.

GRAHAM.   From the presidency? I don't understand.

QUINN.   I don't believe in giant business, or giant government, or giant anything. And the laugh is ... no man has done more to make GE the giant it is today.

GRAHAM.   Well, now! *(He laughs.)* I think this takes us off the financial section and onto the front page! But tell me, how does a man with your ideas rise so high in a great corporation like this? How did you get into GE?

QUINN.   Well, it's a long story, but I love to tell it. I started
out studying law at night and working as a clerk in a factory that
manufactured bulbs for auto headlights. Y'see, in those days they
had forty or fifty makes of car and all different specifications for
the lightbulbs. Now, say you got an order for five thousand
lamps. The manufacturing process was not too accurate, so you
had to make eight or nine thousand to come out with five thousand perfect ones. Result, though, was that we had hundreds of
thousands of perfectly good lamps left over at the end of the
year. So ... one night on my own time I went through the
records and did some simple calculations and came up with a
new average. My figure showed that to get five thousand good
bulbs we only had to make sixty-two hundred instead of eight
thousand. Result was, that company saved a hundred and thirty
thousand dollars in one year. So the boss and I became very
friendly, and one day he says, "I'm selling out to General Electric," but he couldn't tell whether they'd be keeping me on. So
he says to me, "Ted, tell you what we do. They're coming out
from Wall Street" — these bankers, y'see — "and I'm going to
let you pick them up at the depot." Figuring I'd be the first to
meet them and might draw their attention and they'd rehire me,
y'see. Well, I was just this hick-town kid, y'know, about to meet
these great big juicy Wall Street bankers — I tell you, I hardly
slept all night tryin' to figure how to make an impression. And
just toward dawn ... it was during breakfast — and I suddenly
thought of that wall. See, the factory had this brick wall a block
long; no windows, two stories high, just a tremendous wall of
bricks. And it went through my mind that one of them might
ask me how many bricks were in that wall. 'Cause I could answer any question about the company except that. So I got over
to the plant as quick as I could, multiplied the vertical and hori-
zontal bricks, and got the number. Well ... these three bankers
arrive, and I get them into the boss's limousine, and we ride.
Nobody asks me anything! Three of them in those big fur-lined
coats, and not one goddamn syllable.... Anyway we round the
corner, and doesn't one of them turn to me and say, "Mr.
Quinn, how many bricks you suppose is in that wall!" And by

God, I told him! Well, he wouldn't believe it, got out and counted himself — and it broke the ice, y'see, and one thing and another they made me manager of the plant. And that's how I got into GE.

GRAHAM.   *(Astonished.)* What are your plans? Will you join another company or ...

QUINN.   No. I've been tickling the idea I might set up an advisory service for small business. Say a fella has a concept, I could teach him how to develop and market it ... 'cause I *know* all that, and maybe I could help *(To the audience.)* to keep those individuals coming. Because with this terrible Depression you hear it everywhere now — an individual man is not worth a bag of peanuts. I don't know the answers, Mr. Graham, but I sure as hell know the question: How do you keep everything that's big from swallowing everything that's small? 'Cause when that happens — God Almighty — it's not going to be much fun!

GRAHAM.   Well ... thanks very much. Good day. Good day, Mr. Robertson. I must say...! *(With a broken laugh and a shake of the head, he hurries out.)*

QUINN.   He was not massively overwhelmed, was he?

ROBERTSON.   He heard the gentle clip-clop of the horse and buggy coming down the road.

QUINN.   All right, then, damn it, maybe what you ought to be looking into, Arthur, is horseshoes!

ROBERTSON.   Well, you never did do things in a small way! This is unquestionably the world record for the shortest presidency in corporate history. *(He exits. Alone, Quinn stares around in a moment of surprise and fright at what he's actually done. Soft-shoe music steals up, and he insinuates himself into it, dancing in a kind of uncertain mood that changes to release and joy, and at the climax he sings the last lines of a song like "My Baby Just Cares for Me."* As the lyrics end, the phone rings. He picks up the receiver, never losing the beat, and simply lets it drop, and dances off. Rose comes D., staring front, a book in her hand.)*

ROSE.   Who would believe it? You look out the window in the

---

* See Special Note on copyright page.

middle of a fine October day, and there's a dozen college graduates with advanced degrees playing ball in the street like children. And it gets harder and harder to remember when life seemed to have so much purpose, when you couldn't wait for the morning! *(Lee enters, takes a college catalogue off the prop table, and approaches her, turning the pages.)*

LEE.   At Cornell there's no tuition fee at all if you enroll in bacteriology.

ROSE.   Free *tuition!*

LEE.   Maybe they're short of bacteriologists.

ROSE.   Would you like that?

LEE.   *(Stares, tries to see himself as a bacteriologist, sighs.)* Bacteriology?

ROSE.   *(Wrinkling her nose.)* Must be awful. Is anything else free?

LEE.   It's the only one I've seen.

ROSE.   I've got to finish this before tomorrow. I'm overdue fourteen cents on it.

LEE.   What is it?

ROSE.   *Coronet* by Manuel Komroff. It's about this royal crown that gets stolen and lost and found again and lost again for generations. It's supposed to be literature, but I don't know, it's very enjoyable. *(She goes back to her book.)*

LEE.   *(Closes the catalogue, looks at her.)* Ma?

ROSE.   *(Still reading.)* Hm?

LEE.   *(Gently breaking the ice.)* I guess it's too late to apply for this year anyway. Don't you think so?

ROSE.   *(Turns to him.)* I imagine so, dear ... for this year.

LEE.   Okay, Ma ...

ROSE.   I feel so terrible — all those years we were throwing money around, and now when you need it —

LEE.   *(Relieved, now that he knows.)* That's okay. I think maybe I'll try looking for a job. But I'm not sure whether to look under "Help Wanted, Male" or "Boy Wanted."

ROSE.   Boy! *(Their gazes meet. She sees his apprehension.)* Don't be frightened, darling — you're going to be wonderful! *(She hides her feeling in the book. Fadeout. Light comes up on Fanny, standing on the first-level balcony. She calls to Sidney, who is playing the piano and*

singing a song like "Once in a While."*)
FANNY.   Sidney? *(He continues singing.)* Sidney? *(He continues singing.)* Sidney? *(He continues singing.)* I have to talk to you, Sidney. *(He continues singing.)* Stop that for a minute!
SIDNEY.   *(Stops singing.)* Ma, look ... it's only July. If I was still in high school it would still be my summer vacation.
FANNY.   And if I was the Queen of Rumania I would have free rent. You graduated, Sidney, this is not summer vacation.
SIDNEY.   Mama, it's useless to go to employment agencies — there's grown men there, engineers, college graduates. They're willing to take anything. If I could write one hit song like this, just one — we wouldn't have to worry again. Let me have July, just July — see if I can do it. Because that man was serious — he's a good friend of the waiter who works where Bing Crosby's manager eats. He could give him any song I write, and if Crosby just sang it one time ...
FANNY.   I want to talk to you about Doris.
SIDNEY.   What Doris?
FANNY.   Doris! Doris from downstairs. I've been talking to her mother. She likes you, Sidney.
SIDNEY.   Who?
FANNY.   Her mother! Mrs. Gross. She's crazy about you.
SIDNEY.   *(Not comprehending.)* Oh.
FANNY.   She says all Doris does is talk about you.
SIDNEY.   *(Worried.)* What is she talking about me for?
FANNY.   No, nice things. She likes you.
SIDNEY.   *(Amused, laughs incredulously.)* Doris? She's thirteen.
FANNY.   She'll be fourteen in December. Now listen to me.
SIDNEY.   What, Ma?
FANNY.   It's all up to you, Sidney, I want you to make up your own mind. But Papa's never going to get off his back again, and after Lucille's wedding we can forget about *her* salary. Mrs. Gross says — being she's a widow, y'know? And with her goiter and everything ...
SIDNEY.   What?

* See Special Note on copyright page.

FANNY.   If you like Doris — only if you like her — and you would agree to get married — when she's eighteen, about, or seventeen, even — if you would agree to it now, we could have this apartment rent-free. Starting next month.

SIDNEY.   *(Impressed, even astounded.)* Forever?

FANNY.   Of course. You would be the husband, it would be your house. You'd move downstairs, with that grand piano and the tile shower ... I even think if you'd agree she'd throw in the three months' back rent that we owe. I wouldn't even be surprised you could take over the bakery.

SIDNEY.   The bakery! For God's sake, Mama, I'm a composer!

FANNY.   Now listen to me ... *(Doris enters and sits on the floor weaving a cat's cradle of string.)*

SIDNEY.   But how can I be a baker!

FANNY.   Sidney, dear, did you ever once look at that girl?

SIDNEY.   Why should I look at her!

FANNY.   *(Taking him to the "window.")* Because she's a beauty. I wouldn't have mentioned it otherwise. Look. Look at that nose. Look at her hands. You see those beautiful little white hands? You don't find hands like that everywhere.

SIDNEY.   But Ma, listen — if you just leave me alone for July, and if I write one hit song ... I know I can do it, Mama.

FANNY.   Okay. Sidney, we're behind a hundred and eighty dollars. August first we're out on the street. So write a hit, dear. I only hope that four, five years from now you don't accidentally run into Doris Gross somewhere and fall in love with her — after we all died from exposure!

SIDNEY.   But Ma, even if I agreed — supposing next year or the year after I meet some other girl and I really like her ...

FANNY.   All right, and supposing you marry *that* girl and a year after you meet another girl you like better — what are you going to do, get married every year?... But I only wanted you to know the situation. I'll close the door, everything'll be quiet. Write a big hit, Sidney! *(She exits. Sidney begins to sing a song like "Once in a While"*; Doris echoes him timorously. They trade a few lines,*

* See Special Note on copyright page.

Sidney hesitant and surprised. Then.)

DORIS. *(Fully confident, ending the song.)* "... nearest your heart."

SIDNEY. *(Sits on his heels beside her as she weaves the string.)* Gee, you're really terrific at that, Doris. *(He stands, she stands, and they shyly walk off together as he slips his hand into hers.)*

ROBERTSON. *(From choral area.)* I guess the most shocking thing is what I see from the window of my Riverside Drive apartment. It's Calcutta on the Hudson, thousands of people living in cardboard boxes right next to that beautiful drive. It is like an army encampment down the length of Manhattan Island. At night you see their campfires flickering, and some nights I go down and walk among them. Remarkable, the humor they still have, but of course people still blame themselves rather than the government. But there's never been a society that hasn't had a clock running on it, and you can't help wondering — how long? How long will they stand for this? So now Roosevelt's got in I'm thinking — boy, he'd better move. He'd better move fast.... And you can't help it; first thing every night when I get home, I go to the window and look down at those fires, the flames reflecting off the river through the night. *(Lights come up on Moe and Rose. Moe, in a business suit and hat, is just giving her a peck.)*

ROSE. Goodbye, darling. This is going to be a good day — I know it!

MOE. *(Without much conviction.)* I think you're right. G'bye. *(He walks, gradually comes to a halt. Much uncertainty and tension as he glances back toward his house and then looks down to think. Lee enters, and Rose gives him a farewell kiss. He wears a mackinaw. She hands him a lunch bag.)*

ROSE. Don't squeeze it, I put in some cookies.... And listen — it doesn't mean you can *never* go to college.

LEE. Oh, I don't mind, Ma. Anyway, I like it around machines. I'm lucky I got the job!

ROSE. All the years we had so much, and now when you need it —

LEE. *(Cutting her off.)* See ya! *(He leaves her; she exits. He walks and is startled by Moe standing there.)* I thought you left a long time ago!

MOE.   I'll walk you a way. *(He doesn't bother explaining, simply walks beside Lee, but at a much slower pace than Lee took before. Lee feels his unusual tension but can only glance over at him with growing apprehension and puzzlement. Finally Moe speaks.)* Good job?

LEE.   It's okay. I couldn't believe they picked me!

MOE.   *(Nodding.)* Good. *(They walk on in silence, weaving all over the stage, the tension growing as Lee keeps glancing at Moe, who continuously stares down and ahead as they proceed. At last Moe halts and takes a deep breath.)* How much money've you got, Lee?

LEE.   *(Completely taken aback.)* ... money have I got?

MOE.   *(Indicating Lee's pockets.)* I mean right now.

LEE.   Oh! Well, about ... *(He takes out change.)* ... thirty-five cents. I'm okay.

MOE.   ... Could I have a quarter?... So I can get downtown.

LEE.   *(Pauses an instant, astonished.)* Oh, sure, Pa! *(He quickly searches his pockets again.)*

MOE.   You got your lunch — I'll need a hotdog later.

LEE.   *(Handing him a quarter.)* It's okay. I have a dollar in my drawer.... Should I ... *(He starts to go back.)*

MOE.   No, don't go back. *(He proceeds to walk again.)* Don't, ah ... mention it, heh?

LEE.   Oh, no!

MOE.   She worries.

LEE.   I know. *(To audience.)* We went down to the subway together, and it was hard to look at one another. So we pretended that nothing had happened. *(They come to a halt and sit, as though on a subway.)* But something had.... It was like I'd started to support my *father!* And why that should have made me feel so happy, I don't know, but it did! And to cheer him up I began to talk, and before I knew it I was inventing a fantastic future! I said I'd be going to college in no more than a year, at most two; and that I'd straighten out my mind and become an A student; and then I'd not only get a job on a newspaper, but I'd have my own column, no less! By the time we got to Forty-second Street, the Depression was practically over! *(He laughs.)* And in a funny way it *was* — *(He touches his breast.)* — in here ... even though I knew we had a long bad time ahead of us. And so, like most people, I waited with that crazy kind of expectation that comes when there is no hope, waited for the dream to come back from wherever it had gone to hide. *(A voice from the theatre sings the end of "In New York City, You Really Got to Know Your Line,"* or similar song.)*

END OF ACT ONE

ACT TWO

Rose, at the piano, has her hands suspended over the keyboard as the band pianist plays. She starts singing a song like "He Loves and She Loves,"* then breaks off.

ROSE.   But this piano is not leaving this house. Jewelry, yes, but nobody hocks this dear, darling piano. *(She "plays" and sings more of the song.)* The crazy ideas people get. Mr. Warsaw on our block, to make a little money he started a racetrack in his kitchen, with cockroaches. Keeps them in matchboxes with their names written on — Alvin, Murray, Irving.... They bet nickels, dimes. *(She picks up some sheet music.)* Oh, what a show, that *Funny Face. (She sings the opening of a song like "S'Wonderful."*)* The years go by and you don't get to see a show and Brooklyn drifts further and further into the Atlantic; Manhattan becomes a foreign country, and a year can go by without ever going there. *(She sings more of a song like "S'Wonderful."*)* Wherever you look there's a contest; Kellogg's, Post Toasties, win five thousand, win ten thousand. I guess I ought to try, but the winners are always in Indiana somehow. I only pray to God our health holds up, because one filling and you've got to lower the thermostat for a month. Sing! *(She sings the opening of a song like "Do-Do-Do What You Done-Done-Done Before."*)* I must go to the library — I must start taking out some good books again; I must stop getting so stupid. I don't see anything, I don't hear anything except money, money, money ... *(She "plays" Schumann. Fadeout.)*

ROBERTSON.   *(From choral area.)* Looking back, of course, you can see there were two sides to it — with the banks foreclosing right and left, I picked up some first-class properties for a song. I made more money in the thirties than ever before, or since. But I knew a generation was coming of age who would never

---

* See Special Note on copyright page.

feel this sense of opportunity.

LEE.   After a lot of jobs and saving, I did get to the university, and it was a quiet island in the stream. Two pairs of socks and a shirt, plus a good shirt and a mackinaw, and maybe a part-time job in the library, and you could live like a king and never see cash. So there was a distinct reluctance to graduate into that world out there ... where you knew nobody wanted you. *(Joe, Ralph, and Rudy gather in graduation caps and gowns.)* Joey! Is it possible?

JOE.   What?

LEE.   You're a dentist!

RALPH.   Well, I hope things are better when you get out, Lee.

LEE.   You decide what to do?

RALPH.   There's supposed to be a small aircraft plant still working in Louisville ...

LEE.   Too bad you picked propellers for a specialty.

RALPH.   Oh, they'll make airplanes again — soon as there's a war.

LEE.   How could there be another war?

JOE.   Long as there's capitalism, baby.

RALPH.   There'll always be war, y'know, according to the Bible. But if not, I'll probably go into the ministry.

LEE.   I never knew you were religious.

RALPH.   I'm sort of religious. They pay pretty good, you know, and you get your house and a clothing allowance ...

JOE.   *(Comes to Lee, extending his hand in farewell.)* Don't forget to read Karl Marx, Lee. And if you're ever in the neighborhood with a toothache, look me up. I'll keep an eye out for your byline.

LEE.   Oh, I don't expect a newspaper job — papers are closing all over the place. Drop me a card if you open an office.

JOE.   It'll probably be in my girl's father's basement. He promised to dig the floor out deeper so I can stand up ...

LEE.   What about equipment?

JOE.   I figure two, three years I'll be able to open, if I can make a down payment on a used drill. Come by, I'll put back those teeth Ohio State knocked out.

LEE.   I sure will!... So long, Rudy!

RUDY.   Oh, you might still be seeing me around next semester.

JOE.   You staying on campus?

RUDY.   I might for the sake of my root canals. If I just take one university course I'm still entitled to the Health Service — could get my canals finished.

LEE.   You mean there's a course in the Lit School you haven't taken?

RUDY.   Yeah, I just found out about it. Roman Band Instruments.

JOE.   *(Laughs.)* You're kiddin'!

RUDY.   No, in the Classics Department. Roman Band Instruments. *(He pulls his cheek back.)* See, I've still got three big ones to go on this side. *(Laughter.)* Well, if you really face it, where am I running? Chicago's loaded with anthropologists. Here, the university's like my mother — I've got free rent, wash dishes for my meals, get my teeth fixed, and God knows, I might pick up the paper one morning and there's an ad: "Help Wanted: Handsome young college graduate, good teeth, must be thoroughly acquainted with Roman band instruments"! *(Laughter. They sing a song like "Love and a Dime"* accompanied by Rudy on banjo.)*

RALPH.   I'll keep looking for your by-line anyway, Lee.

LEE.   No, I doubt it; but I might angle a job on a Mississippi paddleboat when I get out.

RUDY.   They still run those?

LEE.   Yeah, there's a few. I'd like to retrace Mark Twain's voyages.

RUDY.   Well, if you run into Huckleberry Finn —

LEE.   I'll give him your regards. *(Laughing, Ralph and Rudy start out.)*

RALPH.   Beat Ohio State, kid!

JOE.   *(Alone with Lee, gives him a clenched-fist salute.)* So long, Lee.

LEE.   *(Returning the salute.)* So long, Joe! *(With fist still clenched, he mimes pulling a whistle, dreamily imagining the Mississippi.)* Toot! Toot! (He moves to a point, taking off his shirt, with which he wipes

---

* See Special Note on copyright page.

sweat off his face and neck as in the distance we hear a paddleboat's engines and wheel in water and whistle. Lee stares out as though from a deck. He is seeing aloud.) How scary and beautiful the Mississippi is. How do they manage to live? Every town has a bank boarded up, and all those skinny men sitting on the sidewalks with their backs against the storefronts. It's all stopped; like a magic spell. And the anger, the anger ... when they were handing out meat and beans to the hungry, and the maggots wriggling out of the beef, and that man pointing his rifle at the butcher demanding the fresh meat the government had paid him to hand out.... How could this have happened, is Marx right? Paper says twelve executives in tobacco made more than thirty thousand farmers who raised it. How long can they accept this? The anger has a smell, it hangs in the air wherever people gather.... Fights suddenly break out and simmer down. Is this when revolution comes? And why not? How would Mark Twain write what I have seen? Armed deputies guarding cornfields and whole families sitting beside the road, staring at that food which nobody can buy and is rotting on the stalk. It's insane. *(He exits.)*

ROSE. *(From choral area, to audience.)* But how can he become a sportswriter if he's a Communist? *(Joe, carrying a large basket of flowers, crosses D. to the sound effect of a subway train passing. He sings a verse of a song like "In New York City, You Really Got to Know Your Line."* He then breaks U. and enters Isabel's apartment. She is in bed.)*

ISABEL. Hello, honey.

JOE. Could you start calling me Joe? It's less anonymous. *(He starts removing his shoes and top pair of trousers.)*

ISABEL. Whatever you say. You couldn't come later — hey, could you? I was just ready to go to sleep, I had a long night.

JOE. I can't, I gotta catch the girls before they get to the office, they like a flower on the desk. And later I'm too tired.

ISABEL. Ain't that uncomfortable — hey? Two pairs of pants?

JOE. It's freezing cold on that subway platform. The wind's like the Gobi Desert. The only problem is when you go out to

* See Special Note on copyright page.

56

pee it takes twice as long.

ISABEL. Sellin' books too — hey?

JOE. No, I'm reading that. Trying not to forget the English language. All I hear all day is shit, fuck, and piss. I keep meaning to tell you, Isabel, it's so relaxing to talk to you, especially when you don't understand about seventy percent of what I'm saying.

ISABEL. *(Laughs, complimented.)* Hey!

JOE. *(Takes her hand.)* In here I feel my sanity coming back, to a certain extent. Down in the subway all day I really wonder maybe some kind of lunacy is taking over. People stand there waiting for the train, talking to themselves. And loud, with gestures. And the number of men who come up behind me and feel my ass. *(With a sudden drop in all his confidence.)* What scares me, see, is that I'm getting too nervous to pick up a drill — if I ever get to practice dentistry at all, I mean. The city ... is crazy! A hunchback yesterday suddenly comes up to me ... apropos of nothing ... and he starts yelling, "You will not find one word about democracy in the Constitution, this is a Christian Republic!" Nobody laughed. The Nazi swastika is blossoming out all over the toothpaste ads. And it seems to be getting worse — there's a guy on Forty-eighth Street and Eighth Avenue selling two hotdogs for seven cents! What can he make?

ISABEL. Two for *seven?* Jesus.

JOE. I tell you I get the feeling every once in a while that some bright morning millions of people are going to come pouring out of the buildings and just ... I don't know what ... kill each other? Or only the Jews? Or just maybe sit down on the sidewalk and cry. *(Now he turns to her and starts to climb up on the bed beside her.)*

ISABEL. *(Looking at the book.)* It's about families?

JOE. No, it's just called *The Origin of the Family, Private Property, and the State,* by Friedrich Engels. Marxism.

ISABEL. What's that?

JOE. *(His head resting on hers, his hand holding her breast.)* Well, it's the idea that all of our relationships are basically ruled by money.

ISABEL. *(Nodding, as she well knows.)* Oh, right — hey, yeah.

57

JOE. *(Raising himself up.)* No, it's not what you think ...

ISABEL. It's a whole book about *that?*

JOE. It's about socialism, where the girls would all have jobs so they wouldn't have to do this, see.

ISABEL. Oh! But what would the guys do, though?

JOE. *(Flustered.)* Well ... like for instance if I had money to open an office I would probably get married very soon.

ISABEL. Yeah, but I get married guys. *(Brightly.)* And I even get two dentists that you brought me ... Bernie and Allan? ... and they've got offices, too.

JOE. You don't understand.... He shows that underneath our ideals it's all economics between people, and it shouldn't be.

ISABEL. What should it be?

JOE. Well, you know, like ... love.

ISABEL. Ohhh! Well that's nice — hey. You think I could read it?

JOE. Sure, try.... I'd like your reaction. I like you early, Isabel, you look so fresh. Gives me an illusion.

ISABEL. I'm sorry if I'm tired.

JOE. *(Kisses her, trying to rouse himself.)* Say ... did Bernie finish the filling?

ISABEL. Yeah, he polished yesterday.

JOE. Open. *(She opens her mouth.)* Bernie's good. *(Proudly.)* I told you, we were in the same class. Say hello when you see him again.

ISABEL. He said he might come after five. He always says to give you his best.

JOE. Give him my best, too.

ISABEL. *(Readying herself on the bed.)* Till you I never had so many dentists. *(He lowers onto her. Fadeout. Lights come up on Banks, suspended in a painter's cradle, painting a bridge. He sings a verse of a song like "Backbone and Navel Doin' the Belly Rub,"* then speaks.)*

BANKS. Sometimes you'd get the rumor they be hirin' in New York City, so we all went to New York City, but they wasn't

---

* See Special Note on copyright page.

58

nothin' in New York City, so we'd head for Lima, Ohio; Detroit, Michigan; Duluth, Minnesota; or go down Baltimore; or Alabama or Decatur, Illinois. But anywhere you'd go was always a jail. I was in a chain gang in Georgia pickin' cotton for four months just for hoboin' on a train. That was 1935 in the summertime, and when they set me free they give me thirty-five cents. Yes, sir, thirty-five cents is what they give me, pickin' cotton four months against my will. *(Pause.)* Yeah, I still hear that train, that long low whistle, *whoo-ooo! (Fadeout. Lights come up on Rose, seated at the piano, playing. Two moving men in work aprons enter, raise her hands from the piano, and push the piano off.)*

ROSE.   *(Half to herself, furious.)* How stupid it all is. How stupid! *(Prayerfully.)* Oh, my dear Lee, wherever you are — believe in something. Anything. But believe. *(She turns and moves off with the piano stool, as though emptied out. Lights come up on Lee, sitting at an open-air café table under a tree. Isaac, the black proprietor, brings him a watermelon slice.)*

ISAAC.   You been workin' the river long? I ain't seen you before, have I?

LEE.   No, this is my first trip down the river, I'm from New York City — I'm just kind of looking around the country, talking to people.

ISAAC.   What you lookin' around *for?*

LEE.   Nothing — just trying to figure out what's happening. Ever hear of Mark Twain?

ISAAC.   He from round here?

LEE.   Well, long time ago, yeah. He was a story writer.

ISAAC.   Unh-unh. I ain't seen him around here. You ask at the post office?

LEE.   No, but I might. I'm kind of surprised you can get fifteen cents a slice down here these days.

ISAAC.   Ohhh — white folks *loves* watermelon. Things as bad as this up North?

LEE.   Probably not quite. I sure wouldn't want to be one of you people down here ... specially with this Depression.

ISAAC.   Mister, if I was to tell you the God's honest truth, the main thing about the Depression is that it finally hit the white people. 'Cause us folks never had nothin' else. *(He looks offstage.)*

Well, now — here come the big man.

LEE. He trouble?

ISAAC. He's anything he wants to be, mister — he the sheriff. *(The Sheriff enters, wearing holstered gun, boots, badge, broad-brimmed hat, and carrying something wrapped under his arm. He silently stares at Lee, then turns to Isaac.)*

SHERIFF. Isaac?

ISAAC. Yes, sir.

SHERIFF. *(After a moment.)* Sit down.

ISAAC. Yes, sir. *(He sits on a counter stool; he is intensely curious about the Sheriff's calling on him but not frightened. The Sheriff seems to be having trouble with Lee's strange presence.)*

LEE. *(Makes a nervous half-apology.)* I'm off the boat. *(He indicates offstage.)*

SHERIFF. You don't bother me, boy — relax. *(He sits and sets his package down and turns with gravity to Isaac. Lee makes himself unobtrusive and observes in silence.)*

ISAAC. Looks like rain.

SHERIFF. *(Preoccupied.)* Mm ... hard to know.

ISAAC. Yeah ... always is in Louisiana. *(Pause.)* Anything I can do for you, Sheriff?

SHERIFF. Read the papers today?

ISAAC. I couldn't read my name if an air-o-plane wrote it in the sky, Sheriff, you know that.

SHERIFF. My second cousin Allan? The state senator?

ISAAC. Uh-huh?

SHERIFF. The governor just appointed him. He's gonna help run the state police.

ISAAC. Uh-huh?

SHERIFF. He's comin' down to dinner Friday night over to my house. Bringin' his wife and two daughters. I'm gonna try to talk to Allan about a job on the state police. They still paying the *state* police, see.

ISAAC. Uh-huh. Well, that be nice, won't it.

SHERIFF. Isaac, I like you to cook me up some of that magical fried chicken around six o'clock Friday night. Okay? I'll pick it up.

ISAAC. *(Noncommittal.)* Mm.

SHERIFF.   That'd be for ... let's see ... *(Counts on his fingers.)*
... eight people. My brother and his wife comin' over too, 'cause
I aim to give Allan a little spread there, get him talkin' real
good, y'know.
ISAAC.   Mm. *(An embarrassed pause.)*
SHERIFF.   What's that gonna cost me for eight people, Isaac?
ISAAC.   *(At once.)* Ten dollars.
SHERIFF.   Ten.
ISAAC.   *(With a little commiseration.)* That's right, Sheriff.
SHERIFF.   *(Slight pause; starts to unwrap radio.)* Want to show you
something here, Isaac. My radio, see?
ISAAC.   Uh-huh. *(He runs his hand over it.)* Play?
SHERIFF.   Sure! Plays real good. I give twenty-nine ninety-five
for that two years ago.
ISAAC.   *(Looks in the back of it.)* I plug it in?
SHERIFF.   Go right ahead, sure. You sure painted this place up
real nice. Like a real restaurant. You oughta thank the Lord,
Isaac.
ISAAC.   *(Takes out the wire and plugs it in.)* I sure do. The Lord
and fried chicken!
SHERIFF.   You know, the county ain't paid nobody at all in
three months now ...
ISAAC.   Yeah, I know. Where you switch it on?
SHERIFF.   Just turn the knob. There you are. *(He turns it on.)*
They're still payin' the *state* police, see. And I figure if I can get
Allan to put me on — *(Radio music. It is very faint.)*
ISAAC.   Cain't hardly hear it.
SHERIFF.   *(Angrily.)* Hell, Isaac, gotta get the aerial out! *(Un-
tangling a wire at the back of the set.)* You give me eight fried
chicken dinners and I'll let you hold this for collateral, okay?
Here we go now. *(The Sheriff backs away, stretching out the aerial
wire, and Roosevelt's voice suddenly comes on strong. The Sheriff holds
still, the wire held high. Lee is absorbed.)*
ROOSEVELT.   Clouds of suspicion, tides of ill-will and intoler-
ance gather darkly in many places. In our own land we enjoy,
indeed, a fullness of life ...
SHERIFF.   And nice fat chickens, hear? Don't give me any little
old scruffy chickens.

61

ISAAC. *(Of Roosevelt.)* Who's that talkin'?

ROOSEVELT. ... greater than that of most nations. But the rush of modern civilization itself has raised for us new difficulties ...

SHERIFF. Sound like somebody up North.

ISAAC. Hush! *(To Lee.)* Hey, that's Roosevelt, ain't it?

LEE. Yes.

ISAAC. Sure! That's the President!

SHERIFF. How about it, we got a deal? Or not? *(Isaac has his head close to the radio, absorbed. Lee comes closer, bends over to listen.)*

ROOSEVELT. ... new problems which must be solved if we are to preserve in the United States the political and economic freedom for which Washington and Jefferson planned and fought. We seek not merely to make government a mechanical implement, but to give it the vibrant personal character that is the embodiment of human charity. We are poor indeed if this nation cannot afford to lift from every recess of American life the dark fear of the unemployed that they are not needed in the world. We cannot afford to accumulate a deficit in the books of human fortitude. *(Sidney and Doris enter as lights fade on Lee, Isaac, and the Sheriff.)*

SIDNEY. What's the matter? Boy, you can change quicker than ...

DORIS. *(Shaking her head, closing her eyes.)* I can't help it, it keeps coming back to me.

SIDNEY. How can you let a dope like Francey bother you like this?

DORIS. Because she's spreading it all over the class! And I still don't understand how you could have said a thing like that.

SIDNEY. Hon ... all I said was that if we ever got married I would probably live downstairs. Does that mean that that's the reason we'd get married? Francey is just jealous!

DORIS. *(Deeply hurt.)* I just wish you hadn't said that.

SIDNEY. You mean you think I'd do a thing like that for an *apartment?* What must you think of me!...

DORIS. *(Sobs.)* It's just that I love you so much!...

SIDNEY. If I could only sell a song! Or even pass the post office exam. Then I'd have my own money, and all this garbage would stop.

DORIS.   ... I said I love you, why don't *you* say something?

SIDNEY.   I love you, I love you, but I tell ya, you know what I think?

DORIS.   What?

SIDNEY.   Honestly — I think we ought to talk about seeing other people for a while.

DORIS.   *(Uncomprehending.)* What other people?

SIDNEY.   Going out. You're still a little young, honey ... and even at my age, it's probably not a good idea for us if we never even went out with somebody else —

DORIS.   Well, who ... do you want to take out?

SIDNEY.   Nobody!...

DORIS.   Then what do you mean?

SIDNEY.   Well, it's not that I *want* to.

DORIS.   Yeah, but who?

SIDNEY.   Well, I don't know ... like maybe ... what's-her-name, Margie Ganz's sister ...

DORIS.   *(Alarmed.)* You mean Esther Ganz with the... ? *(She cups her hands to indicate big breasts.)*

SIDNEY.   Then *not* her!

DORIS.   *(Hurt.)* You want to take out *Esther Ganz?*

SIDNEY.   I'm not saying *necessarily!* But ... for instance, you could go out with Georgie.

DORIS.   Which Georgie?

SIDNEY.   Georgie Krieger.

DORIS.   You're putting me with *Georgie Krieger* and *you* go out with *Esther Ganz?*

SIDNEY.   It was only an *example!*

DORIS.   *(With incredulous distaste.)* But Georgie *Krieger!*...

SIDNEY.   Forget Georgie Krieger! Make it ... all right, *you* pick somebody, then.

DORIS.   *(Stares, reviewing faces.)* Well ... how about Morris?

SIDNEY.   *(Asking the heart-stopping question.)* What Morris? You mean Morris from ...

DORIS.   Yeah, Morris from the shoe store.

SIDNEY.   *(Glimpsing quite a different side of her.)* Really?

DORIS.   Well, didn't he go a year to City College?

63

SIDNEY.   No, he did not, he went one semester — and he *still* walks around with a comb in his pocket.... I think maybe we just better wait.

DORIS.   I don't know, maybe it would be a good idea ... at least till I'm a little older ...

SIDNEY.   No, we'll wait, we'll think it over.

DORIS.   But you know ...

SIDNEY.   *(With high anxiety.) We'll think it over,* hon!... *(He goes to the piano, plays a progression. She comes to him, then runs her fingers through his hair.)*

DORIS.   Play "Sittin' Around."

SIDNEY.   It's not any good.

DORIS.   What do you mean, it's your greatest! Please!

SIDNEY.   *(Sighs, sings.)*

> You've got me
> Sittin' around
> Just watching shadows
> On the wall;
> You've got me
> Sittin' around,
> And all my hopes beyond recall;
>
> I want to hear
> The words of love,
> I want to feel
> Your lips on mine,

DORIS.   And know

> The days and nights
> There in your arms.

SIDNEY and DORIS.

> Instead I'm ...
>
> Sittin' around
> And all the world
> Is passing by,
> You've got me
> Sittin' around

Like I was only
Born to cry,

When will I know
The words of love, —
Your lips on mine —
Instead of

Sittin' around,
Sittin' around,
Sittin' around ...

(Fadeout. A large crowd emerges from darkness as a row of factory-type lights descend, illuminating rows of benches and scattered chairs. This is an emergency welfare office temporarily set up to handle the flood of desperate people. A Welfare Worker hands each applicant a sheet of paper and then wanders off.)

MOE.   I don't understand this. I distinctly read in the paper that anybody wants to work can go direct to WPA and they fix you up with a job.

LEE.   They changed it. You can only get a WPA job now if you get on relief first.

MOE.   *(Pointing toward the line.)* So this is not the WPA.

LEE.   I told you, Pa, this is the relief office.

MOE.   Like ... welfare.

LEE.   Look, if it embarrasses you —

MOE.   Listen, if it has to be done it has to be done. Now let me go over it again — what do I say?

LEE.   You refuse to let me live in the house. We don't get along.

MOE.   Why can't you live at home?

LEE.   If I can live at home, I don't need relief. That's the rule.

MOE.   Okay. So I can't stand the sight of you.

LEE.   Right.

MOE.   So you live with your friend in a rooming house.

LEE.   Correct.

MOE.   ... They're gonna believe that?

LEE.   Why not? I left a few clothes over there.

MOE.   All this for twenty-two dollars a week?

LEE. *(Angering.)* What am I going to do? Even old-time news-papermen are out of work.... See, if I can get on the WPA Writers Project, at least I'd get experience if a real job comes along. I've explained this a dozen times, Pa, there's nothing complicated.

MOE. *(Unsatisfied.)* I'm just trying to get used to it. All right. *(They embrace.)* We shouldn't look too friendly, huh?

LEE. *(Laughs.)* That's the idea!

MOE. I don't like you, and you can't stand the sight of me.

LEE. That's it! (*He laughs.*)

MOE. *(To the air, with mock outrage.)* So he laughs. *(They move into the crowd and find seats in front of Ryan, the supervisor, at a desk.)*

RYAN. Matthew R. Bush! *(A very dignified man of forty-five rises, crosses, and follows Ryan out.)*

MOE. Looks like a butler.

LEE. Probably was.

MOE. *(Shakes his head mournfully.)* Hmm!

ROBERTSON. *(From choral area.)* I did a lot of walking back in those days, and the contrasts were startling. Along the West Side of Manhattan you had eight or ten of the world's greatest ocean liners tied up — I recall the SS *Manhattan,* the *Berengaria,* the *United States* — most of them would never sail again. But at the same time they were putting up the Empire State Building, highest in the world. But with whole streets and avenues of empty stores who would ever rent space in it? *(A baby held by Grace, a young woman in the back, cries. Moe turns to look, then stares ahead.)*

MOE. Lee, what'll you do if they give you a pick-and-shovel job?

LEE. I'll take it.

MOE. You'll dig holes in the streets?

LEE. It's no disgrace, Dad.

ROBERTSON. It was incredible to me how long it was lasting. I would never, never have believed we could not recover before this. The years were passing, a whole generation was withering in the best years of its life ... *(The people in the crowd start talking: Kapush, Slavonic, in his late sixties, with a moustache; Dugan, an*

Irishman; Irene, a middle-aged black woman; Toland, a cabbie.)

KAPUSH.   *(With ferocious frustration.)* What can you expect from a country that puts a frankfurter on the Supreme Court? Felix the Frankfurter. Look it up.

DUGAN.   *(From another part of the room.)* Get back in the clock, ya cuckoo!

KAPUSH.   *(Turning his body around angrily to face Dugan and jarring Irene, sitting next to him.)* Who's talkin' to me!

IRENE.   Hey, now, don't mess with me, mister!

DUGAN.   Tell him, tell him! *(Ryan rushes in. He is pale, his vest is loaded with pens and pencils, and a sheaf of papers is in his hand. A tired man.)*

RYAN.   We gonna have another riot, folks? Is that what we're gonna have? Mr. Kapush, I told you three days running now, if you live in Bronx, you've got to apply in Bronx.

KAPUSH.   It's all right, I'll wait.

RYAN.   *(As he passes Dugan.)* Leave him alone, will you? He's a little upset in his mind.

DUGAN.   He's a fascist. I seen him down Union Square plenty of times. *(Irene slams her walking stick down on the table.)*

RYAN.   Oh, Jesus ... here we go again.

IRENE.   Gettin' on to ten o'clock, Mr. Ryan.

RYAN.   I've done the best I can, Irene ...

IRENE.   That's what the good Lord said when he made the jackass, but he decided to knuckle down and try harder. People been thrown out on the sidewalk, mattresses, pots and pans, and everything else they own. Right on A Hundred and Thirty-eighth Street. They goin' back in their apartments today or we goin' raise us some real hell.

RYAN.   I've got no more appropriations for you till the first of the month, and that's it, Irene.

IRENE.   Mr. Ryan, you ain't talkin' to me, you talkin' to Local Forty-five of the Workers Alliance, and you know what that mean.

DUGAN.   *(Laughs.)* Communist Party.

IRENE.   That's right, mister, and they don't mess. So why don't you get on your phone and call Washington. And while you're at it, you can remind Mr. Roosevelt that I done swang One

Hundred and Thirty-ninth Street for him in the last election, and if he want it swung again he better get crackin'!

RYAN. Holy Jesus. *(He hurries away, but Lee tries to delay him.)*

LEE. I was told to bring my father.

RYAN. What?

LEE. Yesterday. You told me to —

RYAN. Get off my back, will ya? *(He hurries out.)*

DUGAN. This country's gonna end up on the top of the trees throwin' coconuts at each other.

MOE. *(Quietly to Lee.)* I hope I can get out by eleven, I got an appointment with a buyer.

TOLAND. *(Next to Moe with a* Daily News *open in his hands.)* Boy, oh, boy, looka this — Helen Hayes gonna put on forty pounds to play Victoria Regina.

MOE. Who's that?

TOLAND. Queen of England.

MOE. She was so fat?

TOLAND. Victoria? Horse. I picked up Helen Hayes when I had my cab. Very small girl. And Adolphe Menjou once — he was small too. I even had Al Smith once, way back before he was governor. He was real small.

MOE. Maybe your cab was extra large.

TOLAND. What do you mean? I had a regular Ford.

MOE. You lost it?

TOLAND. What're you gonna do? The town is walkin'. I paid five hundred dollars for a new Ford, including bumpers and a spare. But thank God, at least I got into the housing project. It's nice and reasonable.

MOE. What do you pay?

TOLAND. Nineteen fifty a month. It sounds like a lot, but we got three nice rooms — providin' I get a little help here. What's your line?

MOE. I sell on commission right now. I used to have my own business.

TOLAND. Used-ta. Whoever you talk to, "I used-ta." If they don't do something, I tell ya, one of these days this used-ta be a country.

KAPUSH. *(Exploding.)* Ignorance, ignorance! People don't know

68

facts. Greatest public library system in the entire world and nobody goes in but Jews.

MOE. *(Glancing at him.)* Ah-ha.

LEE. What're you, Iroquois?

DUGAN. He's a fascist. I seen him talking on Union Square.

IRENE. Solidarity, folks, black and white together, that's what we gotta have. Join the Workers Alliance, ten cents a month, and you git yourself some solidarity.

KAPUSH. I challenge anybody to find the word democracy in the Constitution. This is a republic! *Demos* is the Greek word for mob.

DUGAN. *(Imitating the bird.) Cuckoo!*

KAPUSH. Come to get my money and the bank is closed up! Four thousand dollars up the flue. Thirteen years in hardware, savin' by the week.

DUGAN. Mental diarrhea.

KAPUSH. Mobocracy. Gimme, gimme, gimme, all they know.

DUGAN. So what're *you* doing here?

KAPUSH. Roosevelt was sworn in on a Dutch Bible! *(Silence.)* Anybody know that? *(To Irene.)* Betcha didn't know that, did you?

IRENE. You givin' me a headache, mister ...

KAPUSH. I got nothin' against colored. Colored never took my store away. Here's my bankbook, see that? Bank of the United States. See that? Four thousand six hundred and ten dollars and thirty-one cents, right? Who's got that money? Savin' thirteen years, by the week. *Who's got my money? (He has risen to his feet. His fury has turned the moment silent. Matthew Bush enters and sways. Ryan enters.)*

RYAN. *(Calls.)* Arthur Clayton!

CLAYTON. *(Starts toward Ryan from the crowd and indicates Bush.)* I think there's something the matter with — *(Bush collapses on the floor. For a moment no one moves. Then Irene goes to him, bends over him.)*

IRENE. Hey. Hey, mister. *(Lee helps him up and sits him in the chair.)*

RYAN. *(Calling.)* Myrna, call the ambulance! *(Irene lightly slaps Bush's cheeks.)*

LEE. You all right?

RYAN. *(Looking around.)* Clayton?

CLAYTON. I'm Clayton.

RYAN. *(Clayton's form in his hand.)* You're not eligible for re-lief; you've got furniture and valuables, don't you?

CLAYTON. But nothing I could realize anything on.

RYAN. Why not?

IRENE. This man's starvin', Mr. Ryan.

RYAN. What're you, a medical doctor now, Irene? I called the ambulance! Now don't start makin' an issue, will you? *(To Clayton.)* Is this your address? Gramercy Park South?

CLAYTON. *(Embarrassed.)* That doesn't mean a thing. I haven't really eaten in a few days, actually ...

RYAN. Where do you get that kind of rent?

CLAYTON. I haven't paid my rent in over eight months ...

RYAN. *(Starting away.)* Forget it, mister, you got valuables and furniture, you can't —

CLAYTON. I'm very good at figures, I was in brokerage. I thought if I could get anything that required ... say statistics ...

IRENE. Grace? You got anything in that bottle? *(Grace, in a rear row with a baby in her arms, reaches forward with a baby bottle that has an inch of milk at the bottom. She hands the bottle to Irene.)*

GRACE. Ain't much left there ...

IRENE. *(Takes nipple off bottle.)* Okay, now, open your mouth, mister. *(Bush gulps the milk.)* There, look at that, see? Man's starvin'!

MOE. *(Stands, reaching into his pocket.)* Here ... look ... for God's sake. *(He takes out change and picks out a dime.)* Why don't you send down, get him a bottle of milk?

IRENE. *(Calls toward a young woman in the back.)* Lucy?

LUCY. *(Coming forward.)* Here I am, Irene.

IRENE. Go down the corner, bring a bottle of milk. *(Moe gives her the dime, and Lucy hurries out.)* And a couple of straws, honey! You in bad shape, mister — why'd you wait so long to get on relief?

BUSH. Well ... I just don't like the idea, you know.

IRENE. Yeah, I know — you a real bourgeoisie. Let me tell you something —

BUSH. I'm a chemist.

70

IRENE.   I believe it, too — you so educated you sooner die than say brother. Now lemme tell you people. *(Addressing the crowd.)* Time has come to say brother. My husband pass away and leave me with three small children. No money, no work — I's about ready to stick my head in the cookin' stove. Then the city marshal come and take my chest of drawers, bed, and table, and leave me sittin' on a old orange crate in the middle of the room. And it come over me, mister, come over me to get mean. And I got real mean. Go down in the street and start yellin' and howlin' like a real mean woman. And the people crowd around the marshal truck, and 'fore you know it that marshal turn himself around and go on back downtown empty-handed. And that's when I see it. I see the solidarity, and I start to preach it up and down. 'Cause I got me a stick, and when I start poundin' time with this stick, a whole lot of people starts to march, keepin' time. We shall not be moved, yeah, we shall in no wise be disturbed. Some days I goes to court with my briefcase, raise hell with the judges. Ever time I goes into court the cops commence to holler, "Here comes that old lawyer woman!" But all I got in here is some old newspaper and a bag of cayenne pepper. Case any cop start musclin' me around — that hot pepper, that's hot cayenne pepper. And if the judge happen to be Catholic I got my rosary layin' in there, and I kind of let that crucifix hang out so's they think I'm Catholic too. *(She draws a rosary out of her bag and lets it hang over the side.)*

LUCY.   *(Enters with milk.)* Irene!

IRENE.   Give it here, Lucy. Now drink it slow, mister. Slow, slow ... *(Bush is drinking in sips. People now go back into themselves, read papers, stare ahead.)*

RYAN.   Lee Baum!

LEE.   *(Hurries to Moe.)* Here! Okay, Dad, let's go. *(Lee and Moe go to Ryan's desk.)*

RYAN.   This your father?

MOE.   Yes.

RYAN.   *(To Moe.)* Where's he living now?

LEE.   I don't live at home because —

RYAN.   Let *him* answer. Where's he living, Mr. Baum?

MOE.   Well, he ... he rents a room someplace.

RYAN.   You gonna sit there and tell me you won't let him in the house?

MOE.   *(With great difficulty.)* I won't let him in, no.

RYAN.   You mean you're the kind of man, if he rang the bell and you opened the door and saw him, you wouldn't let him inside?

MOE.   Well, naturally, if he just wants to come in the house —

LEE.   I don't want to live there —

RYAN.   I don't care what *you* want, fella. *(To Moe.)* You will let him into the house, right?

MOE.   *(Stiffening.)* ... I can't stand the sight of him.

RYAN.   Why? I saw you both sitting here talking together the last two hours.

MOE.   We weren't talking.... We were arguing, fighting!...

RYAN.   Fighting about what?

MOE.   *(Despite himself; growing indignant.)* Who can remember? We were fighting, we're always fighting!...

RYAN.   Look, Mr. Baum ... you're employed, aren't you?

MOE.   I'm employed? Sure I'm employed. Here. (He *holds up the folded* Times.) See? Read it yourself. R.H. Macy, right? Ladies' full-length slip, genuine Japanese silk, hand-embroidered with lace top and trimmings, two ninety-eight. My boss makes four cents on these, I make a tenth of a cent. That's how I'm employed!

RYAN.   You'll let him in the house. *(He starts to move.)*

MOE.   I will not let him in the house! He ... he don't believe in anything! *(Lee and Ryan look at Moe in surprise. Moe himself is caught off balance by his genuine outburst and rushes out. Ryan glances at Lee, stamps a requisition form, and hands it to him, convinced. Ryan exits. Lee moves slowly, staring at the form. The welfare clients exit, the row of overhead lights flies out. Lights come up on Robertson.)*

ROBERTSON.   Then and now, you have to wonder what really held it all together, and maybe it was simply the Future: the people were still not ready to give it up. Like a God, it was always worshiped among us, and they could not yet turn their backs on it. Maybe it's that simple. Because from any objective viewpoint, I don't understand why it held. *(The people from the re-*

lief office form a line as on a subway platform. Joe comes behind the line singing and offering flowers from a basket. There is the sound of an approaching train, its windows flashing light. Joe throws himself under it: a squeal of brakes. The crowd sings a song like "In New York City, You Really Got to Know Your Line,"* one by one taking the lyrics, ending in a chorus. Fadeout. Lights come up on Edie. Lee is in spotlight.)

LEE.   *(To audience.)* Any girl with an apartment of her own was beautiful. She was one of the dialogue writers for the *Superman* comic strip. *(To her.)* Edie, can I sleep here tonight?

EDIE.   Oh, hi, Lee — yeah, sure. Let me finish and I'll put a sheet on the couch. If you have any laundry, throw it in the sink. I'm going to wash later. *(He stands behind her as she works.)* This is going to be a terrific sequence.

LEE.   It's amazing to me how you can keep your mind on it.

EDIE.   He's also a great teacher of class consciousness.

LEE.   Superman?

EDIE.   He stands for justice!

LEE.   Oh! You mean under capitalism you can't ...

EDIE.   Sure! The implications are terrific. *(She works lovingly for a moment.)*

LEE.   Y'know, you're beautiful when you talk about politics, your face lights up.

EDIE.   *(Smiling.)* Don't be such a bourgeois horse's ass. I'll get your sheet. *(She starts up.)*

LEE.   Could I sleep in your bed tonight? I don't know what it is lately — I'm always lonely. Are you?

EDIE.   Sometimes. But a person doesn't have to go to bed with people to be connected to mankind.

LEE.   You're right. I'm ashamed of myself.

EDIE.   Why don't you join the Party?

LEE.   I guess I don't want to ruin my chances; I want to be a sportswriter.

EDIE.   You could write for the *Worker* sports page.

LEE.   The *Daily Worker* sports page?

EDIE.   Then help improve it! Why are you so defeatist, hun-

* See Special Note on copyright page.

dreds of people are joining the Party every week.

LEE.   I don't know why, maybe I'm too skeptical — or cynical. Like ... when I was in Flint, Mich'gan, during the sit-down strike. Thought I'd write a feature story ... all those thousands of men barricaded in the GM plant, the wives hoisting food up to the windows in baskets. It was like the French Revolution. But then I got to talk to them as individuals, and the prejudice! The ignorance!... In the Ford plant there was damn near a race war because some of the Negro workers didn't want to join the strike.... It was murderous.

EDIE.   Well, they're still backward, I know that.

LEE.   No, they're normal. I really wonder if there's going to be time to save this country from itself. You ever wonder that? You do, don't you.

EDIE.   *(Fighting the temptation to give way.)* You really want my answer?

LEE.   Yes.

EDIE.   We're picketing the Italian consulate tomorrow, to protest Mussolini sending Italian troops to the Spanish Civil War. Come! *Do* something! You love Hemingway so much, read what he just said — "One man alone is no fucking good." As decadent as he is, even *he's* learning.

LEE.   Really, your face gets so beautiful when you ...

EDIE.   Anyone can be beautiful if what they believe is beautiful! I believe in my comrades. I believe in the Soviet Union. I believe in the working class and the peace of the whole world when socialism comes ...

LEE.   Boy, you really are wonderful. Look, now that I'm on relief can I take you out to dinner? I'll pay, I mean.

EDIE.   *(Smiles.)* Why must you pay for me, just because I'm a woman?

LEE.   Right! I forgot about that.

EDIE.   *(Working.)* I've got to finish this panel.... I'll make up the couch in a minute.... What about the Writer's Project, you getting on?

LEE.   I think so; they're putting people on to write a WPA Guide, it's going to be a detailed history of every section of the country. I might get sent up to the Lake Champlain district.

74

Imagine? They're interviewing direct descendants of the soldiers who fought the Battle of Fort Ticonderoga. Ethan Allen and the Green Mountain Boys?

EDIE.   Oh, yes! They beat the British up there.

LEE.   It's a wonderful project; 'cause people really don't know their own history.

EDIE.   *(With longing and certainty.)* When there's socialism everyone will.

LEE.   *(Leaning over to look at her work.)* Why don't you have Superman get laid? Or married even.

EDIE.   He's much too busy. *(He comes closer to kiss her; she starts to respond, then rejects.)* What are you *doing?*

LEE.   When you say the word "socialism" your face gets so beautiful ...

EDIE.   You're totally cynical, aren't you.

LEE.   Why!

EDIE.   You pretend to have a serious conversation when all you want is to jump into my bed; it's the same attitude you have to the auto workers ...

LEE.   I can't see the connection between the auto workers and...!

EDIE.   *(Once again on firm ground.)* Everything is connected! I have to ask you to leave!

LEE.   Edie!

EDIE.   You are not a good person! *(She bursts into tears and rushes off.)*

LEE.   *(Alone, full of remorse.)* She's right, too! *(He exits. Grandpa enters from choral area, sits with his newspaper, and is immediately immersed. Then Rose's niece Lucille, her sister Fanny, and Doris, who wears a bathrobe, carry folding chairs and seat themselves around a table. Lucille deals cards. Now Rose begins speaking within the choral area, and as she speaks, she moves onto the stage proper.)*

ROSE.   That endless Brooklyn July! That little wooden house baking in the heat. *(She enters the stage.)* I never smelled an owl, but in July the smell of that attic crept down the stairs, and to me it smelled as dry and dusty as an owl. *(She surveys the women staring at their cards.)* From Coney Island to Brooklyn Bridge, how many thousands of women waited out the afternoons dreaming

75

at their cards and praying for luck? Ah, luck, luck ...

DORIS. Sidney's finishing a beautiful new song, Aunt Rose.

ROSE. *(Sitting at the table, taking up her hand of cards.)* Maybe this one'll be lucky for you. Why are you always in a bathrobe?

DORIS. I'm only half a block away.

ROSE. But you're so young! Why don't you get dressed and leave the block once in a while?

FANNY. *(Smugly.)* All my girls love it home, too.

ROSE. *(Indicates the cards.)* It's you, isn't it?

FANNY. *(Brushing dandruff off her bosom and nervously examining her cards.)* I'm trying to make up my mind.

ROSE. Concentrate. Forget your dandruff for a minute.

FANNY. It wasn't dandruff, it was a thread.

ROSE. Her dandruff is threads. It's an obsession.

LUCILLE. I didn't tell you; this spring she actually called me and my sisters to come and spend the day cleaning her house.

FANNY. What's so terrible! We used to have the most marvelous times the four of us cleaning the house ... *(Suddenly.)* It's turning into an oven in here.

LUCILLE. I'm going to faint.

ROSE. Don't faint, all the windows are open in the back of the house. We're supposed to be away.

FANNY. But there's no draft.... For Papa's sake ...

LUCILLE. Why couldn't you be away and you left a window open?... Just don't answer the door.

ROSE. I don't want to take the chance. This one is a professional collector, I've seen him do it; if a window's open he tries to listen. They're merciless.... I sent Stanislaus for lemons, we'll have cold lemonade. Play.

FANNY. I can't believe they'd actually evict you, Rose.

ROSE. You can't? Wake up, Fanny. It's a bank — may they choke after the fortune of money we kept in there all those years! Ask them for two hundred dollars now and they ... *(Tears start to her eyes.)*

FANNY. Rose, dear, come on — something'll happen, you'll see. Moe's got to find something soon, a man so well known.

LUCILLE. Couldn't he ask his mother for a little?

ROSE. His mother says there's a Depression going on. Meantime you can go blind from the diamonds on her fingers. Which he gave her! The rottenness of people! I tell you, the next time I start believing in anybody or anything I hope my tongue is cut out!

DORIS.   Maybe Lee should come back and help out?

ROSE.   Never! Lee is going to think his own thoughts and face the facts. He's got nothing to learn from us. Let him help himself.

LUCILLE.   But to take up Communism —

ROSE.   Lucille, what do you know about it? What does anybody know about it? The newspapers? The newspapers said the stock market will never come down again.

LUCILLE.   But they're against God, Aunt Rose.

ROSE.   I'm overjoyed you got so religious, Lucille, but please for God's sake don't tell me about it again!

FANNY.   *(Rises, starts to leave.)* I'll be right down.

ROSE.   Now she's going to pee on her finger for luck.

FANNY.   All right! So I won't go! *(She returns to her chair.)* And I wasn't going to pee on my finger!

ROSE.   So what're we playing — cards or statues? *(Doris sits looking at her cards, full of confusion.)*

GRANDPA.   *(Putting down his paper.)* Why do they need this election?

ROSE.   What do you mean, why they need this election?

GRANDPA.   But everybody knows Roosevelt is going to win again. I still think he's too radical, but to go through another election is a terrible waste of money.

ROSE.   What are you talking about, Papa — it's four years, they have to have an election.

GRANDPA.   Why! If they decided to make him king ...

ROSE.   King!

FANNY.   *(Pointing at Grandpa, agreeing and laughing.)* Believe me!

GRANDPA.   If he was king he wouldn't have to waste all his time making these ridiculous election speeches, and maybe he could start to improve things!

ROSE.   If I had a stamp I'd write him a letter.

GRANDPA.   He could be another Kaiser Franz Joseph. Then after he dies you can have all the elections you want.

ROSE. *(To Doris.)* Are you playing cards or hatching an egg?

DORIS. *(Startled.)* Oh, it's my turn? *(She turns a card.)* All right; here!

ROSE. Hallelujah. *(She plays a card. It is Lucille's turn; she plays.)* Did you lose weight?

LUCILLE. I've been trying. I'm thinking of going back to the carnival. *(Doris quickly throws an anxious look toward Grandpa, who is oblivious, reading.)*

FANNY. *(Indicating Grandpa secretively.)* You better not mention ...

LUCILLE. He doesn't have to know, and anyway I would never dance anymore; I'd only assist the magician and tell a few jokes. They're talking about starting up again in Jersey.

ROSE. Herby can't find anything?

LUCILLE. He's going out of his mind, Aunt Rose.

ROSE. God Almighty. So what's it going to be, Fanny?

FANNY. *(Feeling rushed, studying her cards.)* One second! Just let me figure it out.

ROSE. When they passed around the brains this family was out to lunch.

FANNY. It's so hot in here I can't think!

ROSE. Play! I can't open the window. I'm not going to face that man again. He has merciless eyes. *(Stanislaus, a middle-aged seaman in T-shirt and dungarees, enters through the front door.)* You come in the front door? The mortgage man could come today!

STANISLAUS. I forgot! I didn't see anybody on the street, though. *(He lifts bag of lemons.)* Fresh lemonade coming up on deck. I starched all the napkins. *(He exits.)*

ROSE. Starched all the napkins ... they're cracking like matzos. I feel like doing a fortune. *(She takes out another deck of cards, lays out a fortune.)*

LUCILLE. I don't know, Aunt Rose, is it so smart to let this man live with you?

DORIS. I would never dare! How can you sleep at night with a strange man in the cellar?

FANNY. Nooo! Stanislaus is a gentleman. *(To Rose.)* I think he's a little bit a fairy, isn't he?

ROSE. I hope! *(They all laugh.)* For God's sake, Fanny, play the queen of clubs!

FANNY.   How did you know I had the queen of clubs!

ROSE.   Because I'm smart, I voted for Herbert Hoover. I see what's been played, dear, so I figure what's left.

FANNY.   *(To Grandpa, who continues reading.)* She's a marvel, she's got Grandma's head.

ROSE.   Huh! Look at this fortune.

FANNY.   Here, I'm playing. *(She plays a card.)*

ROSE.   *(Continuing to lay out the fortune.)* I always feed the vagrants on the porch, but Stanislaus, when I hand him a plate of soup he says he wants to wash the windows before he eats. *Before!* That I never heard. I nearly fell over. Go ahead, Doris, it's you.

DORIS.   *(Desperately trying to be quick.)* I know just what to do, wait a minute. *(The women freeze, study their cards; Rose now faces front. She is quickly isolated in light.)*

ROSE.   When I went to school we had to sit like soldiers, with backs straight and our hands clasped on the desk; things were supposed to be upright. When the navy came up the Hudson River, you cried it was so beautiful. You even cried when they shot the Czar of Russia. He was also beautiful. President Warren Gamaliel Harding, another beauty. Mayor James J. Walker smiled like an angel, what a nose, and those tiny feet. Richard Whitney, president of the Stock Exchange, a handsome, upright man. I could name a hundred from the rotogravure! Who could know that these upright handsome men would either turn out to be crooks who would land in jail or ignoramuses? What is left to believe? The bathroom. I lock myself in and hold on to the faucets so I shouldn't scream. At my husband, my mother-in-law, at God knows what until they take me away ... *(Returning to the fortune, and with deep anxiety.)* What the hell did I lay out here? What is this? *(Light returns to normal.)*

DORIS.   "Gray's Elegy in a Country Churchyard."

ROSE.   What?

FANNY.   *(Touching her arm worriedly.)* Why don't you lie down, Rose?...

ROSE.   Lie down?... Why? *(To Doris.)* What Gray's "Elegy"? What are you ... *(Stanislaus enters rapidly, wearing a waist-length white*

79

starched waiter's jacket, a tray expertly on his shoulder, with glasses and rolled napkins. Rose shows alarm as she lays a card down on the fortune.)

STANISLAUS.   It's a braw bricht moonlicht nicht tonicht — that's Scotch.

FANNY.   How does he get those napkins to stand up!

ROSE.   *(Under terrific tension, tears her gaze from the cards she laid out.)* What's the jacket suddenly? *(The women watch her tensely.)*

STANISLAUS.   *(Saluting.)* SS *Manhattan*. Captain's steward at your service.

ROSE.   Will you stop this nightmare? Take the jacket off. What're you talking about, captain's steward? Who are you?

STANISLAUS.   I was captain's personal steward, but they're not sailing the *Manhattan* anymore. Served J. Pierpont Morgan, John D. Rockefeller, Enrico Caruso, lousy tipper, Lionel —

ROSE.   *(Very suspiciously.)* Bring in the cookies, please. *(He picks up the pitcher to pour the lemonade.)* Thank you, I'll pour it. Go, please. *(She doesn't look at him; he goes out. In the silence she picks up the pitcher, tilts it, but her hand is shaking, and Fanny takes the pitcher)*

FANNY.   Rose, dear, come upstairs ...

ROSE.   How does he look to you?

FANNY.   Why? He looks very nice.

LUCILLE.   He certainly keeps the house beautiful, Aunt Rose, it's like a ship.

ROSE.   He's a liar, though; anything comes into his head, he says; what am I believing him for? What the hell got into me? You can tell he's full of shit, and he comes to the door, a perfect stranger, and I let him sleep in the cellar!

LUCILLE.   *Shhh! (Stanislaus enters with a plate of cookies, in T-shirt again, determinedly.)*

ROSE.   Listen, Stanislaus ... *(She stands.)*

STANISLAUS.   *(Senses his imminent dismissal.)* I go down to the ship chandler store tomorrow, get some special white paint, paint the whole outside the house. I got plenty of credit, don't cost you.

ROSE.   I thought it over, you understand?

STANISLAUS. *(With a desperate smile.)* I borrow big ladder from the hardware store. And I gonna make nice curtains for the cellar windows. Taste the lemonade, I learn that in Spanish submarine. Excuse me, gotta clean out the icebox. *(He gets himself out.)*
FANNY.   I think he's very sweet, Rose.... Here ... *(She offers a glass of lemonade.)*
LUCILLE.   Don't worry about that mortgage man, Aunt Rose, it's after five, they don't come after five ...
ROSE.   *(Caught in her uncertainty.)* He seems sweet to you?
GRANDPA.   *(Putting the paper down.)* What Lee ought to do ... Rosie?
ROSE.   Hah?
GRANDPA.   Lee should go to Russia. *(The sisters and Lucille turn to him in surprise.)*
ROSE.   *(Incredulous, frightened.)* To Russia?
GRANDPA.   In Russia they need everything; whereas here, y'see, they don't need anything, so therefore, there's no work.
ROSE.   *(With an edge of hysteria.)* Five minutes ago Roosevelt is too radical, and now you're sending Lee to Russia?
GRANDPA.   That's different. Look what it says here ... a hundred thousand American people applying for jobs in Russia. Look, it says it. So if Lee would go over there and open up a nice chain of clothing stores —
ROSE.   Papa! You're such a big anti-Communist ... and you don't know the government owns everything in Russia?
GRANDPA.   Yeah, but not the *stores.*
ROSE.   Of course the stores!
GRANDPA.   The *stores* they own?
ROSE.   Yes!
GRANDPA.   Them bastards.
ROSE.   *(To Lucille.)* I'll go out of my mind here ...
DORIS.   So who wrote it?
ROSE.   Wrote what?
DORIS.   "Gray's Elegy in a Country Churchyard." It was a fifteen-dollar question on the radio yesterday, but you were out. I ran to call you.
ROSE.   *(Suppressing a scream.)* Who wrote Gray's "Elegy in a Country Churchyard"?

DORIS.   By the time I got back to the radio it was another question.

ROSE.   Doris, darling ... (*Slowly.*) Gray's "Elegy in a — *(Fanny laughs.)* What are you laughing at, do you know?

FANNY.   *(Pleasantly.)* How would I know?

LUCILLE.   Is it Gray? *(Rose looks at her, an enormous sadness in her eyes. With a certain timidity, Lucille goes on.)* Well, it says "Gray's Elegy," right?

DORIS.   How could it be Gray? That's the title! *(Rose is staring ahead in an agony of despair.)*

FANNY.   What's the matter, Rose?

DORIS.   Well, what'd I say?

FANNY.   Rose, what's the matter?

LUCILLE.   You all right?

FANNY.   *(Really alarmed, turning Rose's face to her.)* What is the matter! *(Rose bursts into tears. Fanny gets up and embraces her, almost crying herself.)* Oh, Rosie, please ... don't. It'll get better, something's got to happen ... *(A sound from the front door galvanizes them. A man calls from off: "Hello?")*

DORIS.   *(Pointing.)* There's some —

ROSE.   *(Her hands flying up in fury.)* Sssh! *(Whispering.)* I'll go upstairs. I'm not home. *(She starts to go; Moe enters.)*

DORIS.   *(Laughing.)* It's Uncle Moe!

MOE.   What's the excitement?

ROSE.   *(Going to him.)* Oh, thank God, I thought it was the mortgage man. You're home early. *(He stands watching her.)*

FANNY.   Lets go, come on. *(They begin to clear table of tray, lemonade, glasses, etc.)*

MOE.   *(Looking into Rose's face.)* You crying?

LUCILLE.   How's it in the city?

ROSE.   Go out the back, huh?

MOE.   The city is murder.

FANNY.   Will you get your bills together? I'm going downtown tomorrow. I'll save you the postage.

ROSE.   Take a shower. Why are you so pale?

LUCILLE.   Bye-bye, Uncle Moe.

MOE.   Bye, girls.

DORIS.   *(As she exits with Fanny and Lucille.)* I must ask him how he made that lemonade ... *(They are gone, Moe is staring at some vision, quite calm, but absorbed.)*

ROSE. You ... sell anything?... No, heh? *(He shakes his head negatively — but that is not what he is thinking about.)* Here ... *(She gets a glass from the table.)* Come drink, it's cold. *(He takes it but doesn't drink.)*

MOE. You're hysterical every night.

ROSE. No, I'm all right. It's just all so stupid, and every once in a while I can't ... I can't ... *(She is holding her head.)*

MOE. The thing is.... You listening to me?

ROSE. What? *(Suddenly aware of her father's pressure on Moe, she turns and goes quickly to him.)* Go on the back porch, Papa, huh? It's shady there now ... *(She hands him a glass of lemonade.)*

GRANDPA. But the man'll see me.

ROSE. It's all right, he won't come so late, and Moe is here. Go ... *(Grandpa starts to go.)* ... and why don't you put on your other glasses, they're much cooler. *(Grandpa is, gone. She returns to Moe.)* Yes, dear. What. What's going to be?

MOE. We are going to be all right.

ROSE. Why?

MOE. Because we are. So this nervousness every night is unnecessary, and I wish to God —

ROSE. *(Indicating the table and the cards spread out.)* It's just a fortune. I ... I started to do a fortune, and I saw ... a young man. The death of a young man.

MOE. *(Struck.)* You don't say.

ROSE. *(Sensing.)* Why? *(He turns front, amazed, frightened.)* Why'd you say that?

MOE. Nothing ...

ROSE. Is Lee ...

MOE. Will you cut that out —

ROSE. Tell me!

MOE. I saw a terrible thing on the subway. Somebody jumped in front of a train.

ROSE. Aaaahhh — again! My God! You saw him?

MOE. No, a few minutes before I got there. Seems he was a very young man. One of the policemen was holding a great big basket of flowers. Seems he was trying to sell flowers.

ROSE. I saw it! *(Her spine tingling, she points down at the cards.)* Look, it's there! That's death! I'm going to write Lee to come home immediately. I want you to put in that you want him home.

MOE. I have nothing for him, Rose; how can I make him come home?

ROSE. *(Screaming and weeping.)* Then go to your mother and stand up like a man to her ... instead of this goddamned fool! *(She weeps.)*

MOE. *(Stung, nearly beaten, not facing her.)* This can't ... it can't go on forever, Rose, a country can't just die! *(She goes on weeping; he cries out in pain.)* Will you stop? I'm trying! God Almighty, I am trying! *(The doorbell rings. They start with shock. Grandpa enters, hurrying, pointing.)*

GRANDPA. Rose —

ROSE. Ssssh! *(The bell rings again. Moe presses stiffened fingers against his temple, his eyes averted in humiliation. Rose whispers.)* God in heaven ... make him go away! *(The bell rings again. Moe's head is bent, his hand quivering as it grips his forehead.)* Oh, dear God, give our new President the strength, and the wisdom ... *(Door knock, a little more insistent.)* ... give Mr. Roosevelt the way to help us ... *(Door knock.)* Oh, my God, help our dear country ... and the people!... *(Door knock. Fadeout. Lights come up on company as the distant sound of a fight crowd is heard and a clanging bell signals the end of a round. Sidney enters in a guard's uniform; he is watching Lee, who enters smoking a cigar stub, wearing a raincoat, finishing some notes on a pad, his hat tipped back on his head.)*

SIDNEY. Good fight tonight, Mr. Baum.

LEE. *(Hardly glancing at him.)* Huh? Yeah, pretty good. *(Sidney looks on, amused, as Lee slowly passes before him, scribbling away. As Banks speaks, Soldiers appear and repeat italicized words after him.)*

BANKS. When the *war* came I was so *glad* when I got in the *army*. A man could be *killed* anytime at all on those trains, but with that uniform on I said, "Now I am safe."

SIDNEY. Hey!

LEE. Huh? *(Now he recognizes Sidney.)* Sidney!

SIDNEY. Boy, you're some cousin. I'm looking straight at you and no recognito! I'm chief of security here.

BANKS.   I felt proud to salute and look around and see all the *good soldiers* of the United States. I was a good *soldier too,* and got five battle stars. *(Other Soldiers repeat, "Five, five, five.")*

LEE.   You still on the block?

SIDNEY.   Sure. Say, you know who'd have loved to have seen you again? Lou Charney.

LEE.   Charney?

SIDNEY.   Hundred yard dash — you and him used to trot to school together ...

LEE.   Oh, Lou, sure! How is he!

SIDNEY.   He's dead. Got it in Italy.

BANKS.   Yeah, I seen all kinds of war — including the kind they calls ...

COMPANY.   ... peace. *(Four soldiers sing the beginning of a song like "We're in the Money."*)*

SIDNEY.   And you knew Georgie Rosen got killed, didn't you?

LEE.   Georgie Rosen.

SIDNEY.   Little Georgie. Sold you his racing bike. That got stolen.

LEE.   Yes, yes! God — Georgie too.

COMPANY.   *(Whispering.)* Korea.

SIDNEY.   Lot of wars on that block. *(One actor sings the first verse of a song like "The Times They Are A 'Changing."*)* Oh, yeah — Lou Charney's kid was in *Vietnam. (The company says "Vietnam" with Sidney.)* Still and all, it's a great country, huh?

LEE.   Why do you say that?

SIDNEY.   Well, all the crime and divorce and whatnot. But one thing about people like us, you live through the worst, you know the difference between bad and *bad.*

BANKS.   One time I was hoboin' through that high country — the Dakotas, Montana — I come to the monument for General Custer's last stand, Little Big Horn. And I wrote my name on it, yes, sir. For the memories; just for the note; so my name will be up there forever. Yes, sir ...

SIDNEY.   But I look back at it all now, and I don't know about you, but it seems it was friendlier. Am I right?

_____
* See Special Note on copyright page.

LEE.   I'm not sure it was friendlier. Maybe people just cared more.

SIDNEY.   *(With Irene singing a song like "I Want to Be Happy"* under his speech.)* Like the songs, I mean — you listen to a thirties song, and most of them are so happy, and still — you could cry.

BANKS.   But I still hear that train sometimes; still hear that long low whistle. Yes, sir, I still hear that train ... *whoo-ooo!*

LEE.   You still writing songs?

SIDNEY.   Sure! I had a couple published. I got a new one now, though — love you to hear it. I'm calling it "A Moon of My Own." I don't know what happened, I'm sitting on the back porch and suddenly it came to me — "A Moon of My Own." I ran in and told Doris, she could hardly sleep all night. *(Doris quietly sings under the following speeches: " ... and know the days and nights there in your arms. Instead I'm sittin' around ...")*

LEE.   How's Doris, are you still ...

SIDNEY.   Oh, very much so. In fact, we were just saying we're practically the only ones we know didn't get divorced.

LEE.   Did I hear your mother died?

SIDNEY.   Yep, Fanny's gone. I was sorry to hear about Aunt Rose, and Moe.

LEE.   *(Over a song like "Life Is Just a Bowl of Cherries"* music.)* After all these years I still can't settle with myself about my mother. In her own crazy way she was so much like the country. *(Rose sings the first line of a song like "Life Is Just a Bowl of Cherries."* Through the rest of Lee's speech, she sings the next four lines.)* There was nothing she believed that she didn't also believe the opposite. *(Rose sings.)* She'd sit down on the subway next to a black man *(Rose sings.)* and in a couple of minutes she had him asking her advice *(Rose sings.)* about the most intimate things in his life. *(Rose sings.)* Then, maybe a day later —

LEE and ROSE.   "Did you hear! They say the colored are moving in!"

LEE.   Or she'd lament her fate as a woman —

ROSE and LEE.   "I was born twenty years too soon!"

* See Special Note on copyright page.

ROSE.   They treat a woman like a cow, fill her up with a baby and lock her in for the rest of her life.

LEE.   But then she'd warn me, "Watch out for women — when they're not stupid, they're full of deceit." I'd come home and give her a real bath of radical idealism, and she was ready to storm the barricades; by evening she'd fallen in love again with the Prince of Wales. She was so like the country; money obsessed her, but what she really longed for was some kind of height where she could stand and see out and around and breathe in the air of her own free life. With all her defeats she believed to the end that the world was meant to be better.... I don't know; all I know for sure is that whenever I think of her, I always end up — with this headful of life!

ROSE.   *(Calls, in a ghostly, remote way.)* Sing! *(Alternating lines, Lee and Rose sing a song like "Life Is Just a Bowl of Cherries."* The whole company takes up the song in a soft, long-lost tonality. Robertson moves forward, the music continuing underneath.)*

ROBERTSON.   There were moments when the word "revolution" was not rhetorical. *(Ted Quinn steps forward.)*

QUINN.   Roosevelt saved them; came up at the right minute and pulled the miracle.

ROBERTSON.   Up to a point; but what really got us out of it was the war.

QUINN.   Roosevelt gave them back their belief in the country. The government belonged to them again!

ROBERTSON.   Well, I'll give you that.

QUINN.   Of course you will, you're not a damned fool. The return of that belief is what saved the United States, no more, no less!

ROBERTSON.   I think that's putting it a little too ...

QUINN.   *(Cutting him off and throwing up his hands.)* That's it!... God, how I love that music! *(He breaks into his soft-shoe dance as the singing grows louder. He gestures for the audience to join in, and the company does so as well as the chorus swells ...)*

END

* See Special Note on copyright page.

PROPERTY PLOT

Shoeshine box (CLARENCE)
Baseball
Baseball glove
Telephone (MOE, CLAYTON, QUINN)
Diamond bracelet (ROSE)
Crystal set (LEE)
Baggage
Canes (GRANDPA)
Grandpa's hat (ROSE)
Brandy decanter
3 brandy cups
A layer of five-thousand-dollar bills (ROBERTSON)
Bicycle (LEE)
Purse (ROSE)
Pawnshop business card (ROSE)
Photograph of Herbert Hoover (JOEY)
Envelope for Herbert photo (JOEY)
Lap robe (FRANK)
Pram filled with junk (IRENE)
Hatboxes (GRANDPA)
Bed sheet (ROSE
Pearl choker (ROSE)
Coffeepot (MRS. TAYLOR)
Coffee mugs (HARRIET)
Clipboard (MR. HOWARD)
Shotguns (DEPUTIES)
Noose
Bundle of clothes (BANKS)
Cooking pot (BANKS)
College catalogues (LEE)
Paper bag (creased) (TAYLOR)
Dish towel (ROSE)
Glass of water (LEE)

Tray (ROSE) with:
    bowl of soup with spoon
    bread
2 or 3 dollar bills (MOE)
Plum (GRANDPA)
Boater (QUINN)
Cane (QUINN)
Book (ROSE)
String (DORIS)
Lunch bag for Lee (ROSE)
Change (coins) (LEE, MOE)
Sheet music (ROSE)
Banjo (RUDY)
Large basket of flowers (JOE)
Book (JOE)
Watermelon slice (ISAAC)
Radio, wrapped (SHERIFF)
Sheaf of papers to distribute (WELFARE WORKER, RYAN)
Pens and pencils (RYAN)
Baby bottle with inch of milk (GRACE)
Bag (IRENE)
Rosary (IRENE)
Bottle of milk (LUCY)
Newspapers
New York *Times* (MOE)
Rubber stamp (RYAN)
Registration form (RYAN)
Cards (LUCILLE, ROSE)
Bag of lemons (STANISLAUS)
Tray (STANISLAUS) with:
    glasses
    rolled napkins
Pitcher of lemonade (STANISLAUS)
Plate of cookies (STANISLAUS)
Cigar stub (LEE)
Note pad (LEE)
Pencil or pen (LEE)

SITTIN' AROUND

Moderate bounce

Sidney: YOU'VE GOT ME SITTIN' AROUND   JUST WATCHING SHADOWS
ON THE WALL;   YOU'VE GOT ME   SITTIN' AROUND,
AND ALL MY HOPES BEYOND RECALL;   I WANT TO
HEAR THE WORDS OF   LOVE, I WANT TO   FEEL YOUR LIPS   ON
MINE, Doris: AND   KNOW THE DAYS AND   NIGHTS THERE IN YOUR
ARMS.   Both: INSTEAD I'M... SITTIN' AROUND
AND ALL THE WORLD IS   PASSING BY,   YOU'VE GOT ME
SITTIN' AROUND   LIKE I WAS ONLY   BORN TO CRY,
WHEN WILL   I   KNOW THE WORDS OF   LOVE, WHEN WILL I
FEEL YOUR LIPS   ON   MINE ── INSTEAD OF SITTIN' AROUND,   SITTIN'
AROUND, SITTIN' AROUND...

NEW PLAYS

★ THE CREDEAUX CANVAS by Keith Bunin. A forged painting leads to tragedy among friends. "There is that moment between adolescence and middle age when being disaffected looks attractive. Witness the enduring appeal of Prince Hamlet, Jake Barnes and James Dean, on the stage, page and screen. Or, more immediately, take a look at the lithe young things in THE CREDEAUX CANVAS..." –*NY Times.* "THE CREDEAUX CANVAS is the third recent play about painters...it turned out to be the best of the lot, better even than most plays about non-painters." –*NY Magazine.* [2M, 2W] ISBN: 0-8222-1838-0

★ THE DIARY OF ANNE FRANK by Frances Goodrich and Albert Hackett, newly adapted by Wendy Kesselman. A transcendently powerful new adaptation in which Anne Frank emerges from history a living, lyrical, intensely gifted young girl. "Undeniably moving. It shatters the heart. The evening never lets us forget the inhuman darkness waiting to claim its incandescently human heroine." –*NY Times.* "A sensitive, stirring and thoroughly engaging new adaptation." –*NY Newsday.* "A powerful new version that moves the audience to gasps, then tears." –*A.P.* "One of the year's ten best." –*Time Magazine.* [5M, 5W, 3 extras] ISBN: 0-8222-1718-X

★ THE BOOK OF LIZ by David Sedaris and Amy Sedaris. Sister Elizabeth Donderstock makes the cheese balls that support her religious community, but feeling unappreciated among the Squeamish, she decides to try her luck in the outside world. "...[a] delightfully off-key, off-color hymn to clichés we all live by, whether we know it or not." –*NY Times.* "Good-natured, goofy and frequently hilarious..." –*NY Newsday.* "...[THE BOOK OF LIZ] may well be the world's first Amish picaresque...hilarious..." –*Village Voice.* [2M, 2W (doubling, flexible casting to 8M, 7W)] ISBN: 0-8222-1827-5

★ JAR THE FLOOR by Cheryl L. West. A quartet of black women spanning four generations makes up this hilarious and heartwarming dramatic comedy. "...a moving and hilarious account of a black family sparring in a Chicago suburb..." –*NY Magazine.* "...heart-to-heart confrontations and surprising revelations...first-rate..." –*NY Daily News.* "...unpretentious good feelings...bubble through West's loving and humorous play..." –*Star-Ledger.* "...one of the wisest plays I've seen in ages...[from] a master playwright." –*USA Today.* [5W] ISBN: 0-8222-1809-7

★ THIEF RIVER by Lee Blessing. Love between two men over decades is explored in this incisive portrait of coming to terms with who you are. "Mr. Blessing unspools the plot ingeniously, skipping back and forth in time as the details require...an absorbing evening." –*NY Times.* "...wistful and sweet-spirited..." –*Variety.* [6M] ISBN: 0-8222-1839-9

★ THE BEGINNING OF AUGUST by Tom Donaghy. When Jackie's wife abruptly and mysteriously leaves him and their infant daughter, a pungently comic reevaluation of suburban life ensues. "Donaghy holds a cracked mirror up to the contemporary American family, anatomizing its frailties and miscommunications in fractured language that can be both funny and poignant." –*The Philadelphia Inquirer.* "...[A] sharp, eccentric new comedy. Pungently funny...fresh and precise..." –*LA Times.* [3M, 2W] ISBN: 0-8222-1786-4

★ OUTSTANDING MEN'S MONOLOGUES 2001–2002 and OUTSTANDING WOMEN'S MONOLOGUES 2001–2002 edited by Craig Pospisil. Drawn exclusively from Dramatists Play Service publications, these collections for actors feature over fifty monologues each and include an enormous range of voices, subject matter and characters. MEN'S ISBN: 0-8222-1821-6 WOMEN'S ISBN: 0-8222-1822-4

DRAMATISTS PLAY SERVICE, INC.
440 Park Avenue South, New York, NY 10016 212-683-8960 Fax 212-213-1539
postmaster@dramatists.com www.dramatists.com

NEW PLAYS

★ **A LESSON BEFORE DYING by Romulus Linney, based on the novel by Ernest J. Gaines.** An innocent young man is condemned to death in backwoods Louisiana and must learn to die with dignity. "The story's wrenching power lies not in its outrage but in the almost inexplicable grace the characters must muster as their only resistance to being treated like lesser beings." *–The New Yorker.* "Irresistable momentum and a cathartic explosion…a powerful inevitability." *–NY Times.* [5M, 2W] ISBN: 0-8222-1785-6

★ **BOOM TOWN by Jeff Daniels.** A searing drama mixing small-town love, politics and the consequences of betrayal. "…a brutally honest, contemporary foray into classic themes, exploring what moves people to lie, cheat, love and dream. By BOOM TOWN's climactic end there are no secrets, only bare truth." *–Oakland Press.* "…some of the most electrifying writing Daniels has ever done…" *–Ann Arbor News.* [2M, 1W] ISBN: 0-8222-1760-0

★ **INCORRUPTIBLE by Michael Hollinger.** When a motley order of medieval monks learns their patron saint no longer works miracles, a larcenous, one-eyed minstrel shows them an outrageous new way to pay old debts. "A lightning-fast farce, rich in both verbal and physical humor." *–American Theatre.* "Everything fits snugly in this funny, endearing black comedy…an artful blend of the mock-formal and the anachronistically breezy…A piece of remarkably dexterous craftsmanship." *–Philadelphia Inquirer.* "A farcical romp, scintillating and irreverent." *–Philadelphia Weekly.* [5M, 3W] ISBN: 0-8222-1787-2

★ **CELLINI by John Patrick Shanley.** Chronicles the life of the original "Renaissance Man," Benvenuto Cellini, the sixteenth-century Italian sculptor and man-about-town. Adapted from the autobiography of Benvenuto Cellini, translated by J. Addington Symonds. "[Shanley] has created a convincing Cellini, not neglecting his dark side, and a trim, vigorous, fast-moving show." *–BackStage.* "Very entertaining…With brave purpose, the narrative undermines chronology before untangling it…touching and funny…" *–NY Times.* [7M, 2W (doubling)] ISBN: 0-8222-1808-9

★ **PRAYING FOR RAIN by Robert Vaughan.** Examines a burst of fatal violence and its aftermath in a suburban high school. "Thought provoking and compelling." *–Denver Post.* "Vaughan's powerful drama offers hope and possibilities." *–Theatre.com.* "[The play] doesn't put forth compact, tidy answers to the problem of youth violence. What it does offer is a compelling exploration of the forces that influence an individual's choices, and of the proverbial lifelines—be they familial, communal, religious or political—that tragically slacken when society gives in to apathy, fear and self-doubt…" *–Westword.* "…a symphony of anger…" *–Gazette Telegraph.* [4M, 3W] ISBN: 0-8222-1807-0

★ **GOD'S MAN IN TEXAS by David Rambo.** When a young pastor takes over one of the most prestigious Baptist churches from a rip-roaring old preacher-entrepreneur, all hell breaks loose. "…the pick of the litter of all the works at the Humana Festival…" *–Providence Journal.* "…a wealth of both drama and comedy in the struggle for power…" *–LA Times.* "…the first act is so funny…deepens in the second act into a sobering portrait of fear, hope and self-delusion…" *–Columbus Dispatch.* [3M] ISBN: 0-8222-1801-1

★ **JESUS HOPPED THE 'A' TRAIN by Stephen Adly Guirgis.** A probing, intense portrait of lives behind bars at Rikers Island. "…fire-breathing…whenever it appears that JESUS is settling into familiar territory, it slides right beneath expectations into another, fresher direction. It has the courage of its intellectual restlessness…[JESUS HOPPED THE 'A' TRAIN] has been written in flame." *–NY Times.* [4M, 1W] ISBN: 0-8222-1799-6

DRAMATISTS PLAY SERVICE, INC.
440 Park Avenue South, New York, NY 10016 212-683-8960 Fax 212-213-1539
postmaster@dramatists.com www.dramatists.com

NEW PLAYS

★ **THE CIDER HOUSE RULES, PARTS 1 & 2 by Peter Parnell, adapted from the novel by John Irving.** Spanning eight decades of American life, this adaptation from the Irving novel tells the story of Dr. Wilbur Larch, founder of the St. Cloud's, Maine orphanage and hospital, and of the complex father-son relationship he develops with the young orphan Homer Wells. "...luxurious digressions, confident pacing...an enterprise of scope and vigor..." *–NY Times.* "...The fact that I can't wait to see Part 2 only begins to suggest just how good it is..." *–NY Daily News.* "...engrossing...an odyssey that has only one major shortcoming: It comes to an end." *–Seattle Times.* "...outstanding...captures the humor, the humility...of Irving's 588-page novel..." *–Seattle Post-Intelligencer.* [9M, 10W, doubling, flexible casting] PART 1 ISBN: 0-8222-1725-2 PART 2 ISBN: 0-8222-1726-0

★ **TEN UNKNOWNS by Jon Robin Baitz.** An iconoclastic American painter in his seventies has his life turned upside down by an art dealer and his ex-boyfriend. "...breadth and complexity...a sweet and delicate harmony rises from the four cast members...Mr. Baitz is without peer among his contemporaries in creating dialogue that spontaneously conveys a character's social context and moral limitations..." *–NY Times.* "...darkly funny, brilliantly desperate comedy...TEN UNKNOWNS vibrates with vital voices." *–NY Post.* [3M, 1W] ISBN: 0-8222-1826-7

★ **BOOK OF DAYS by Lanford Wilson.** A small-town actress playing St. Joan struggles to expose a murder. "...[Wilson's] best work since *Fifth of July*...An intriguing, prismatic and thoroughly engrossing depiction of contemporary small-town life with a murder mystery at its core...a splendid evening of theater..." *–Variety.* "...fascinating...a densely populated, unpredictable little world." *–St. Louis Post-Dispatch.* [6M, 5W] ISBN: 0-8222-1767-8

★ **THE SYRINGA TREE by Pamela Gien.** Winner of the 2001 Obie Award. A breathtakingly beautiful tale of growing up white in apartheid South Africa. "Instantly engaging, exotic, complex, deeply shocking...a thoroughly persuasive transport to a time and a place...stun[s] with the power of a gut punch..." *–NY Times.* "Astonishing...affecting ...[with] a dramatic and heartbreaking conclusion...A deceptive sweet simplicity haunts THE SYRINGA TREE..." *–A.P.* [1W (or flexible cast)] ISBN: 0-8222-1792-9

★ **COYOTE ON A FENCE by Bruce Graham.** An emotionally riveting look at capital punishment. "The language is as precise as it is profane, provoking both troubling thought and the occasional cheerful laugh...will change you a little before it lets go of you." *–Cincinnati CityBeat.* "...excellent theater in every way..." *–Philadelphia City Paper.* [3M, 1W] ISBN: 0-8222-1738-4.

★ **THE PLAY ABOUT THE BABY by Edward Albee.** Concerns a young couple who have just had a baby and the strange turn of events that transpire when they are visited by an older man and woman. "An invaluable self-portrait of sorts from one of the few genuinely great living American dramatists...rockets into that special corner of theater heaven where words shoot off like fireworks into dazzling patterns and hues." *–NY Times.* "An exhilarating, wicked...emotional terrorism." *–NY Newsday.* [2M, 2W] ISBN: 0-8222-1814-3

★ **FORCE CONTINUUM by Kia Corthron.** Tensions among black and white police officers and the neighborhoods they serve form the backdrop of this discomfiting look at life in the inner city. "The creator of this intense...new play is a singular voice among American playwrights...exceptionally eloquent..." *–NY Times.* "...a rich subject and a wise attitude." *–NY Post.* [6M, 2W, 1 boy] ISBN: 0-8222-1817-8

DRAMATISTS PLAY SERVICE, INC.
440 Park Avenue South, New York, NY 10016 212-683-8960 Fax 212-213-1539
postmaster@dramatists.com www.dramatists.com